MEMORIES AND HOPE

THE ROAD I TRAVELED

By
Guillermina Connor

TEACH Services, Inc.
P U B L I S H I N G
www.TEACHServices.com

Copyright © 2007, 2011 Guillermina Connor
ISBN-13: 978-1-57258-489-1 (Paperback)
ISBN-13: 978-1-57258-957-5 (E-book)
Library of Congress Control Number: 2007935242

Published by
TEACH Services, Inc.
P U B L I S H I N G
www.TEACHServices.com

CONTENTS

DEDICATION

I dedicate this story to the glory of God, the Father, Creator of the Universe in honor of His Son, who died to redeem me from my sins, who has gone to prepare a place for me, and who has promised to come again and take me with Him to live for ever in Glory. I love and adore His Excellent and Marvelous name forever... Jesus Christ, He is my Strength and Salvation.

SOMEONE SPECIAL: with gratitude for their love and support, I thank my devoted mother, grandmother, and friend Ercilia and Georgina, and beautiful family, Tomas, Eloise, America, Edgar.

My delightful husband Albert and to my faithful, respectful, loving and caring children: Tomas, Eduardo, Armando, Olimpia, Ruperta, Elvia, Susana, Guillermina, Margarita and Terrell, and all of my grand children and great grand children in one way or the other, they have all shown their love to me.

INTRODUCTION

My story is a story about the triumph of hope over human experience. A story of one life rescued by the GOD of Heaven, who plucked me from a world of sin and misery, and lifted me up to a life of peace, joy and happiness.

I found CHRIST at the side of the road, and my life was changed forever to a life of faith. Faith is believing and accepting God's promises without any reservation. Faith is talking to God as you would to a friend and hope for an answer. Faith is a simple trust and confidence in the unknown, and in what you cannot prove. My faith has encouraged me to yearn to hear God pronounce, "here are the patience of the saints, here are they who keep the commandments of God, and the faith of Jesus." My determination in life is to be committed to God's will and to proclaim what He has done for me, and what He will do for you.

CHAPTER 1

One Summer evening during my senior years, I sat alone on the corridor at home, appreciating and admiring the handiwork of the Monarch of the Universe. I enjoyed many blessings of a spiritual, physical and material nature that had been granted to my family. Suddenly my dimmed eyes caught a glimpse of the most thrilling and glorious sunset ever seen in the west.

Such a sunset, brings us harmoniously to the revealed will of God throughout the phenomenal world He designed. It also brought back to my mind scenes of one of my old family's customs.

As a child, my parents and siblings would watch the sunset from our back porch on Goat Hill. It was something special, and we looked forward to sharing it together after a long day of household chores were completed. This was a moment for relaxing before the family was tucked in bed.

During our lifetimes, we often hold on to things from our past. Watching the sunset each evening was such a habit that I just could not have forgotten. Years later, after my own marriage and having young ones of my own, I found myself caring and cleaning nine little dirty faces covered with traces of food, sauce and fruits juices (golden mangoes), wiping runny cold noses and messy buttocks, and gently soothing scratched elbows and knees. Yet, I often found myself gathering my family together in the evening on our porch to admire the horizon as the sun disappeared, leaving behind rays of red, yellow, and brown color in the sky.

As I reflected on those glorious mental images, I was inspired to write my own family story. As I describe my family, I would like to single out major Historical events occurring in my parents', siblings, as well as my own life, as well as the story of my family as a whole with its ups and downs due to death, health problems, and my social life. I have chosen to refer to these events "as the special joys of life." But most of all, I want to point to the work of the LORD JESUS CHRIST in my life throughout my story.

Life begins with life" irrespective if we believe life existed before we were born, and will go on without us. Our life is not determined by our genealogy nor where we were born. The fact of the matter is that the Almighty GOD is the creator of life. GOD gave me life, which I have enjoyed for the past eighty years.

In the late 1800s, my ancestor Georgina McKay, a single parent in her mid-twenties, along with her three years old son, William Bucchard, and her brother Henry Bennett, who was in his early thirties, left their homeland of Belize, in the British Honduras to travel to the shores of the Bay Islands of Honduras, Central America. They traveled here mainly for personal reasons. Their arrival was approximately eighteen years after the bay islands became part of the sovereignty of Honduras.

These three brave and courageous individuals were in search of a new life, and they found it on the Island of Roatan. They chose this island as their new home most likely due to its size, which helped to smooth their transition to their new home.

The bay islands are composed of a chain of three large islands: Guanaja, Roatan and Utila, along with a few smaller ones. These islands are located almost thirty-six miles off the Northern Coast of Honduras. Those islands are surrounded by beautiful white sandy beaches, and caressed by crystal clear water from the Caribbean sea. The land is adorned with delicious and desirable tropical bearing fruit trees and colorful flowers.

On October 12, 1492, these breathtaking Bay Islands of Honduras made history when the Spanish Almirant of the sea, Christopher Columbus and his crew, set their anchor on the shore of Guanaja in the New world. Years later, in the mid 1500s, the Englishman Captain Francis Drake captured the islands and drove the Spaniards off the islands, in an attempt to expand the British Emperor. This land remained part of the Englishman's sovereign until April 21, 1861, when they were returned to the Republic of Honduras. They were given in exchange for the Republic of Belize, which had been a colony of Honduras for many years. This was the beginning of an ongoing traffic of immigrants of all ages between Belize and Honduras. My ancestors were among the numerous families of different ethnic background to come to the islands, where they started lives afresh, and began a new generation.

The McKay-Andrew, Bennett and Bucchard family arrived on the Island of Roatan and settled initially in the Town of Coxen Hole. They lived here for some time before being separated due Henry Bennett employment. It must have been a thrilling experience for them, as they most likely faced the greatest challenge of their lives in a country they knew little about. Little did they knew that the country they arrived in was being ravaged by civil wars due to political, economic and social changes.

Georgina and Henry were most likely experiencing second thoughts about their decision to leave their homeland, and probably felt frustrated and restless as a result of the uncertainty they faced. No doubt they were homesick, and longed for the warmth and affection of the loved ones they had left behind. This adjustment to their new home was not easy, but God saw them through their transition.

Those three individuals Georgina, Henry and Williams, eventually became my grandmother and uncles. They were like any other average family that had come to Coxen Hole, yet they had exceptional courage, perseverance and bravery. I have always admired my relatives for their spirit of adventure. At some point in our lives, we too must take the risk of adventuring in hopes of a new start.

Grandmother Georgina's spirit of adventure must have been influenced by the Nineteenth century in which she was born. It was a century that had changed world power. For example, two major events took place in the Latin America and some Caribbean Islands, as they fought for independence from Spain. After 327 years of Spanish reign, most were liberated around September 15, 1821. There was also a religious movement that took place during this time period. In North America, a group of Christians came together, and the Seventh-day Adventist denomination came into existence on October 22, 1844.

My grandmother was a marvelous and extraordinary woman. She was a woman of medium height, brown hair, eyes and skin. She possessed special characteristics that made her outstanding in her neighborhood. She was intelligent, amicable and got along well with the neighbors and anybody she met. She had a big heart. She always would put the needs of others before her own, even when they coincided with hers. She was very skillful in sewing and cooking, and that no doubt made her very popular on the island.

One thing that always intrigued me about my grandmother, was her ability to keep her past life a secret. She was willing to put herself into situations that might be caused by her silence. She never disclosed what her life was before coming to Honduras, nor did she even by mistake mention the name of her son's father. Yet, she was willing to assume the care of an infant child that was brought to her. This child was named Ercilia Andrew-McKay, who later became my mother. My grandmother enjoyed being around families. Her past life memories may have been too painful to talk about, so she kept silent.

Uncle Henry was of medium height, a bit on the chubby side, with black hair, eyes and brown skin. He was a soft spoken person, a carpenter and a sailor by trade. One of his life dreams was to sail on the angry billows, discovering new horizons. He did.

Last but not least was William Buchard, better known as little Willie or Uncle Bill. He was a six-year-old child, handsome with dimples on both cheeks. He had black hair, clear brown eyes and brunet skin. He too later on was motivated to go to sea as like Uncle Henry.

These three individuals, soon adjusted to their new home. They struggled with daily living, doing the best they could to survive during the first few years on the island. As believers in God, Grandma and Uncle Henry trusted Him to provide for all their needs. Suddenly, doors began opening for them. Grandma soon began making a living by sewing for people in the community, including the military force, which was one of her biggest clientèle. Unfortunately, Uncle Henry did not find the same fortune. He was unable to engage in a stable job. He worked at part time carpenter work and odds jobs, but he was never able to earn enough money to contribute to the household or to make his dream of forming a family a reality.

One day, Grandma and Uncle Henry received information from friends living in Jonesville, (on the East side of the island) that a few men were building boats and were looking for an extra hand. After giving it some thought, the family decided that Uncle Henry would take this chance, and travel to Jonesville to explore the possibility of joining these boat constructors. It turned out to be a good move. Things seemed to start looking bright for Uncle Henry, and he also had the chance to make his dream of becoming a sailor come true.

This was the first time that they would be separated from each other since coming to Honduras. It was not an easy decision, but it had to be made. Uncle Henry promised his sister and nephew that he would visit them regularly. It is quite possible that some nostalgic feelings may have aroused in both grandma and Uncle Henry. Yet they both trusted in the God of Heaven, where they found the strength to cope with the separation.

Some days later, my uncle left for Jonesville and was blessed. He found work, and he also found love. After a few years, Uncle Henry got married to a native from the area named Arabella Bodden, a relative of

Teofilo Bodden, who later became my father. My uncle and his new wife never had children of their own, but they adopted his wife's relatives' children. Uncle Henry started his life at sea as a sailor. He sailed from island to island along the northern coast of Honduras picking up cargo loads of copra, bananas, and plantains. These were taken to Jacksonville, Florida. He was a sailor until he retired.

Uncle Henry and Aunt Bella lived to a good old age before he passed on in 1911. Little was known about my Aunt Bella, except that she was short, had chubby dark skin, and resembled an Indian. After Uncle Henry's death, Aunt Bella was taken care of by their adoptive children until her death. Grandma claimed that she had some difficulty dealing with Uncle's death. Her last blood relative was gone, and she felt very alone. I had a similar experience in my own life. I too felt alone when my husband died on December 31, 1961.

Grandma was a very strong woman, and with the help of God, she was able to continue with her life with her son Willie and Chila, her adopted child. Grandma, Willie and Chila continued to be there for each other. Chila was now nine years old, and Willie was 15 years old. In 1891, Grandma had been approached by a young lady from the town of Flowers Bay, who offered her daughter to Grandma. To Grandma this was a dream come true. She had always wanted a little girl to call her own, and even though she did not verbalize this wish, her facial expression exposed her true inner feelings.

According to Grandma, Chila was about a year old when she came to live with her. By calculating what details she knew about Chila, it appears she was born on January 1, 1890. During those years it is not clear if any accurate vital records were kept prior to the 1900s on the island, yet there is a possibility that they were destroyed during the annual winds that swept the islands.

Grandma described Chila as a chubby, attractive, alert and friendly child. She admired Chila's physical beauty. Chila also resembled the Arawak Indian, but this did not bother grandma. It was not clear why Chila's biological mother gave her to grandma. Maybe she was young and had no financial means of support for her daughter, or perhaps her family pressured her to give the child up. She may have brought shame and embarrassment on her family for being an unwed mother.

In those days, a young unwed woman was considered a failure to the parents, and her female siblings would be labeled. Chila's mother never maintained any contact with Chila's birth mother, nor did any of her relatives.

Grandma did not let that bother her. She was glad to have that bundle of joy to loved and care for. Chila brought great joy to grandma's life by filling her emptiness, and this joy spilled over, touching all her family and friends. I'm not aware if my grandma was involved romantically with any other person other than Willie's father, but one could assume that two things might have happened. Either Grandma was holding on to a past love life with Willie's father, and refused to bury the moments she had with Buchard, or the experience of the first marriage was so painful that she was unwilling to let any other person into her life that might touch that pain.

Grandma was not a person who would willingly share her life story with anyone, yet she allowed people to assume. When Grandma accepted Chila into her life, her son Willie was six years older than Chila. He resented Chila getting all the attention, and he felt left out. It took Willie some time before he fully accepted Chila as part of his family. Grandma made sure that Willie and Chila were never left alone. She feared that Willie might take his resentment out on the baby. As a means of precaution, she would always put Chila in a basket and place her on the table next to her sewing machine, where she could watch each of Chila's movements. It also allowed her to protect Chila from Willie's grabbing or twisting her fingers.

Grandma made changes in her busy work schedule, especially at night. She had to temporarily reduce her hours of sewing on most nights to care for Chila. Grandma did not mind the sacrifices she made for Chila. She was her company. and a blessing sent to her by God to complete the McKay's family. Chila was an adorable baby, who did not give many problems, except when she crawled around in the house. She often got between grandma's feet, and hindered her movements. As a teenager, however, Chila became defiant. She was searching for her own identity, and wanted to make her own decisions.

As the years went by Willie grew fond of his adopted sister, and they bonded. Both Willie and Chila attended the same public school, Minerva Elementary, at different years. However, Chila was not as successful with books like Willie because she spent most of her time helping Grandma who couldn't do without her, and was unable to hire anyone at that time. Grandma needed all the help she could get in that house. When Willie and Chila were old enough to help with sewing on a button, or the hemming of a garment, they were drafted into Grandma's business.

During the years as Chila grew up, there was an understanding among the people in the community that girls should be encouraged to be mothers, and take care of the domestic chores. Grandma also had the same opinion. The rationale for this strong belief was that a women's place was in the home.

Chila did not advance in school, but this did not discourage her because she already knew what she wanted in life. Chila did a great job of taking care of the domestic chores. She enjoyed cooking. She had dreams for the future like most young ladies, that one day she would own her own business of a "cook-house," which she did. But her dream was put on hold, when she fell in love and soon after became a teenage parent.

Grandma wanted only the best for her two children, and she was very protective of both of them. In her neighborhood, she was known as the "protective sewing woman." Grandma's goal was only to make sure that Chila especially was protected from the wolves in her days. It only worked for a while until Chila met Thomas Connor, and they fell in love with each other.

Grandma was not too thrilled about the relationship. She adamantly opposed and attempted to separate Chila and Thomas forever, but she was not successful because Chila and Thomas' love was so strong that it made them both deaf and blind to any parental   threat. They ignored all threats and discouragement from Grandma. Almost all of the time, the more protective parents are with their children, the more defiant their children can be. I was also too protective of my children, especially my girls as they were growing up. I was sometimes referred to as "The old hen" or "Lozano." I made sure that the roosters in their times did not attack my brood.

Chila and Thomas' love affair ended up with Chila getting pregnant, and shortly abandoned by the man she adored after her son was born. When Grandma became aware of Chila' pregnancy, she was disappointed and enraged when she learned that Thomas had refused to marry her daughter. In those day an unwed woman brought shame and stigma to the family.

Grandma had preached daily to Chila and Thomas about children born out of wedlock. She said to them that it was morally wrong to have children before marriage. Grandma was right. She had plans for Chila's future. She would have loved to see her one day walk down the church's isles wearing a custom made bridal gown, and holding on to the arm of a gentleman. Now her dream was shattered. This situation might have caused Grandma to remember her personal experiences along with having to see Chila emotionally torn apart and silently suffering when Thomas disappeared from her life and unborn child.

On November 29,1904, it was a rainy day when Chila's first son was born, and she named him after his father, Thomas, who did not stay around long enough to help with the care of his son. They called the little fellow Tommy and they were fond of him. As a young single parent, Chila was aware of her responsibilities to her son. She took pride and care for him with some help from Grandma and Uncle Willie. She also helped grandma with her sewing.

Chila as a conscientious mother, had a strong belief in self support as well as Grandma did. Both ladies came up with an idea to develop a plan that would help to provide additional income to help with her son's daily needs. They decided that Chila could provide meals, and sell them to a handful of individuals.

Chila tried her hand at that project, which eventually blossomed into a community business. As a result, grandma built an extra room onto her home in order to accommodate the numerous customers. Chila was an excellent cook, and the location of the business contributed largely to its success.

Grandma's house was near to the municipal building, the penal center, the park, dentist office, doctor office, criminal judge office and a half block away from the market. Coxen Hole was a little community. Everyone knew their neighbors, and what went on in the community, and Chila's business was no exception. Years later, when Chila moved her business on the top of Goat Hill, it grew and became a historical name in Coxen Hole. Chila's business remained her life's work up until two weeks prior to her passing away on March 29, 1969.

Chila's shop became famous, and was well patronized. It was a place where folks could eat the best home cooked meal in town. The only means of advertisement was, "Each one tell the other." Chila's business served to help her meet distinguished people who visited the island. As a result of this outlet, Chila had the privilege of meeting the President of Honduras, Juan Manuel Galvez, Tiburcio Carias Andino, as well as some some members of their cabinet, during the presidential visits to the Bay Islands.

The news about Chila's shop spread among the islanders, and onto the mainland. It was a surprise how quickly it was accepted by the people, not only because the islands were separated by water, but also because they were populated by various ethnic groups such as the African, Dutch, English, Irish, Italian, Spaniard and Turkish.

Each group had its own cultural practices. Physically, the inhabitants of the island did not resemble the typical Honduran Indian, but we all had the same need for food, shelter and love. Our physical appearance made us unique. It wasn't just our skin pigmentation that made us different, but our surnames were also different from the typical ones. For example, our surnames included Andrew, Arch, Auld, Bodden, Brown, Bush, Campbell, Connor, Dixon, Johnson, Lucas, Litrico, McKay, McBride, Smith, Tatum, Warren, Wilmoth, Woods etc. To our family a name or facial appearance did not matter. The most important thing was that the Lord had chosen to bring us together, and we tried our best to live together in harmony.

On the contrary, the mainland dwellers had a negative perception of the islanders, and referred to us as "coconut eaters", "shrimp eaters" and "conch eaters." The names that were attributed to us did not make us feel inferior or intimidated. Nevertheless, we were proud of our heritage, and who we were. We are a people who are determined to succeed no matter what the obstacles or cost may be.

The inhabitants from the mainland showed how one set of people can be ignorant and prejudiced against other groups. However, their feeling of indifference towards us did not drive them to cause us any physical harm. As the old saying goes, "words can break bones." It is humanly impossible for all people on this planet to share the same physical appearance. When God created mankind, He made a rainbow of races, with ability to share emotions and feelings with another human being.

CHAPTER 2

Despite all the seemingly problems on the islands for Chila, she met two wonderful gentlemen who would have given the world for her if she asked, but the one thing she refused to grant to either of these men was, "The Commitment of Holy Matrimony."

Mr. Teofilo Bodden was and Englishman who was a descendant from the Cayman Island in the Caribbean. He was the first man after Thomas Connor to draw Chila's affection. This relationship was different from the other two. Teofilo Bodden did offer Chila marriage, but Grandma McKay's fear for Chila getting hurt again, had a great influence.

The other gentleman was Antonio Litrico, an Italian (who later became the father of my two sisters America and Eloise). He was originally from Italy, and he loved Chila very much. Yet, he did not proposed to her either.

Perhaps Chila's past, her being a descendant from the Arawack Indian tribe, had something to do with her relationships. The only assumption that comes to mind is that cultural values and believes played a subtle role. Chila benefited from the relationships financially. Chila and her common law husbands lived happily together as long as the relationship lasted. Both men died many years before Chila, but her life choices turned out positive.

In our life's journey on this earth, people make choices. Making choices in life is almost or always difficult. Each one of us, whether young or old, is at the crossroads everyday. The decisions we make determine not only the events of that day, but our life hereafter.

In December 1905, on a cold and winter night, Chila and Teofilo Bodden met for the first time. Uncle Henry had brought Teofilo to visit Grandma's home and Teofilo and Chila fell in love. It was like the movie, "Tarzan met Jane." Teofilo Bodden was a handsome young man, and made a positive impact on Grandma; maybe he reminded her of someone whom she had cared for in the past. He was a sailor like uncle Henry, and they both wore the label of "womanizer."

It is believed that Chila's and Teofilo's meeting was not a coincidence, but part of God's plan for them. I am one hundred percent sure, that my uncle Henry had scrutinized Teofilo for some time, before he decided to bring him along to visit Grandma. Uncle Henry was aware of how particular Grandma was about Chila meeting strangers. She had not forgotten what had happened between Chila and Thomas Connor earlier, and Chila getting to know strangers.

Grandma had great faith in her brother's judgment. She believed that he would not have taken anyone that was not of good character to introduce to her, and she still wanted to make sure that Chila would not get hurt again. Grandma made sure this time that any man who wished to date Chila would prove himself worthy of her hand.

Teofilo Bodden passed the test, with the exception of his occupation. He assured Grandma that he cared and loved Chila so much that he would agree to accept Tommy as his own son, and he would provide financially and spiritually for him, as well as lead him on the right path in life. He promised to teach Tommy to put God first in life. Years later Teofilo became my father.

In addition, Dad agreed to respect Grandma's rules in regards to visitation. It took my father some time before he was able to adjust to Grandma's control over Chila. He eventually gave in, because his love for Chila was stronger than any other obstacle he had to deal with.

One of the major problems that Grandma had with Dad, was his occupation as "sailor." There is an old adage about sailors, which suggests that they have a different woman at every port they visit. Even today, this belief about sailors is still widely circulated.

News about the handsome young man that had come to visit Ms. McKay's daughter spread. My father, better known by his friends and other islanders as the, "Englishman with the English break," proved that he was a one woman man, and that he was stereotypically labeled as a sailor. He told his friends that he had eyes for only Chila, and that he wanted to form a family. Dad and Chila both seemed to be emotionally mature, and continued to build on their relationship.

My father was much older than Chila, and many presumed him to be wiser. However Chila was wiser because of her extensive personal experiences in her life. In general, women reach their mental and emotional maturity much earlier than men.

Dad had had some formal schooling. He knew how to read and write, and he was good in math. Unfortunately, my mother did not have the opportunity to complete even the third grade. She could not read very well, but was extremely good in math, one reasons for her success in business. She was also an industrious woman. Grandma taught Chila domestic chores, and she used these skills whenever the opportunity came. Grandma shaped Chila's life, and she turned out to be a very independent woman even though she was denied an elementary education, which could have helped her personal and intellectual growth.

Three years after my parents were introduced on June 24, 1908, God blessed my parents with a beautiful baby girl who they named Guillermina Georgina Bodden Andrews. This little girl was me. My birth took place in Grandma's home at the foot of Goat Hill. My parents and Grandma were proud of their off spring. I later learned that I was an adorable chubby little girl, with black straight hair like my father's, bright brown eyes and very light skin. As my half brother, I too was born out of wed-lock. This was not because my mother wished it so, but because grandma wanted to hold on to the past, and this created a conflict for my parents. My father was not the kind of person to push an issue, and he would rather follow than create a scene. Dad accepted Grandma's wish, and never pursued marriage. Years went by, and the matter of my parents getting married was forgotten. This gave Grandma the opportunity to keep Chila close by her side.

Grandma had some peculiar motives for doing the things she did. She was not the type of individual who would pour out her heart to anyone, nor was it easy to have a discussion with her. She was, however, a caring and understanding person in her own way. Chila and Dad had their own plan, but their wish was not going to come true until dad was financially secure and able to provide a roof for Chila, Tommy and I. Because of this, they went along with Grandma's caprice, because they did not want to hurt her feelings while Chila lived under her roof. Dad decided to visit Chila, despite Grandma's offering him the right to live in her house, which he later accepted after being encouraged by Chila.

Both Dad and Grandma were proud individuals, and neither wanted to feel like they were doing the other one a favor. Many times, when the weather was bad, my dad risk his health to make sure he kept his promises and spend time with my mother and my brother and I. Dad's love for us was immense as I was his only child, and secondly, I was seen as his old age pension. I was very special, and meant a lot to him.

According to Chila, Dad arrived in Coxen Hole many times either by motor boat or on foot. Sometimes he looked tired and wet. Only the good Lord knew the physical and emotional pains that my parents went through. They had to live separated from each other, and one can assume that it was not easy for a middle aged man.

My parents kept their hope that one day, they would be together. Finally, the great day came when my parents were able to inform Grandma of their plan to construct their own little house on the top of Goat Hill, and establish their own business. Their dream was about to become a reality.

Dad had saved enough money from his time as a sailor, as well as other odd jobs. It was a substantial amount of money, which allowed him to buy the land and to construct his dream house in Coxen Hole for his family. From our home we had a splendid view of the Atlantic Ocean, as well as a view of the homes constructed below. We moved out of Grandma's into our own home. The new inhabitants included, Dad, Chila, Tommy, Don Juan (a family close friend who became as like Chila's adopted son) and myself.

While it should have been a day for rejoicing, it did not happened that way. Grandma did not want to be alone, and she was resentful of my parent's plan. She decided to make a deal with them. The deal was for my parents to leave me with her as her company, and to take Tommy along with them. Dad strongly opposed the idea, but Chila was willing to compromise. After all, Grandma was her mother. However Dad refused to let me stay with Grandma.

We can assume how grandma felt about losing complete control of Chila's life. She was very upset. Chila tried to console Grandma, telling her that we were only moving a few feet away and she was right. The side of the Hill where Grandma lived was not too steep, so she would be able to come and visit our home daily. Grandma might have needed the company, because Willie was at that time residing in Jonesville with uncle Henry and after this move, she was going to be alone.

Shortly after we moved on top of the hill, my parents had the grand opening of their cook house. The opening of the cook house took place on April 21, the same day we celebrated the return of the islands to Honduras also known as Carnival Day. Two months later we had another celebration. On the 24th of June, I was the first one to celebrate a birthday in our new home.

My parents often told us stories about some difficult moments they had the first years they spent on their own and running their own business. My parents both believed in the "Supreme One" who helped them through the difficult times. When I compare the families then and now, I am tempted to believe that families then were some how more dependent on God for their needs. They lived in a time when the joy of living was centered around simplicity; a family, a roof, and no more than bread and water. With these simple blessings, they were happy.

Families then seemed more religious; they were always praising God. I got my first lesson in trusting God to see me through my life struggles and happy moments from my parents. Although most people trust God, some believed in witchcraft. Some of our neighbors practiced voodoo and engaged in putting evil spells on others. Some also claimed to have the ability to transform their body into alligators and threatened to wait for their enemy in certain town on the islands.

One of the woman in the neighborhood had a bad habit of flirting with the men. She did not care whether the man was married or single. One day, this woman became the victim of an evil spell because of her immoral behavior. Her neighbor contracted one of her friends to invite her to a party held in her home, and a special drink was served to her. This drink was suppose to affect her legs with sores. A few days later, rumors spread that the flirtatious woman's legs burst out into painful sores.

At the same time some of this potion helped in curing fever or stomach problems. Therefore, it was not from the potion she drank, but because she did not take care of the sores. There are people who still believe in these stories. But thanks to God, my family did not indulge in this behavior. We have always believed and depended on Him to see us through, and He sure did many times in my own personal life.

My family knew that God was our refuge and strength in times of trouble, as the man of God, David, states in the Bible. We benefited from searching the Holy Word, and everything seemed to go well for us. Dad continued to work as a sailor, while Chila ran the family business. When Dad was on vacation from sailing, Chila would take a little vacation, and Dad would do most of the cooking and cleaning, a job he did well, until it was time for him to return to sea. My Dad made it a habit, for the family to attend Sunday School every week, as long as he was there. Finally, Dad realized that it was somewhat strenuous for Chila alone to take care of the children and run the business. My parents decided that they would hire someone to help with the cooking while my father was away. This went on for few years, until dad retired from his job as a sailor.

During Dad's trips to sea, I was one of the best dressed children in our neighborhood. Dad would either buy dresses or cloth which Chila or Grandma would use to make dresses for me in their spare time. Tommy was always smartly dressed as well.

CHAPTER 3

In the year 1915, one year after World War I had begun in Europe, I turned seven years old. My mother enrolled me in the Minerva Public School, where I was placed in the first grade. Kindergarten and Pre-kindergarten were not available in Roatan at this time. Children who were not of school age, still had an informal preschool experience. They attended weekly gatherings held in homes and churches in the area. These children were taught the alphabet, how to write their names and numerals. They were also taught what is known today as socialization skills, and these skills boasted their self-esteem.

Children were encouraged to behave in a positive manner, both in day-to-day life and in a religious atmosphere. Roatan was a closely knitted community. Our grandparents and elders willingly shared whatever knowledge they had with the younger generations.

Most of the knowledge we acquired at that time, was transmitted orally. We may have been deprived of a formal preschool or kindergarten education, but we did well when we would eventually enter school at the age of seven. My brother was already attending school, and was in the fourth grade when I started school. He was a very bossy older brother, especially when dad and mom were not around. He would force me to do whatever he wanted me to do. For example, he would order me to fetch water or his books. But as I grew older, things began to change.

My first day of school was May 1, 1915. It was a very emotional experience. Chila and I, as well as the other children that were accompanied by their parents, walked into the school yard. We giggled and admired our new clothes, shoes, and cloth bags. I wore a pink dress, pink socks and black shoes. My hair was curled, and I wore pink ribbons. The other children wore beautiful dresses. I remember seeing some children crying, and holding on to their mothers hands when it was time to march into the class room. I was not afraid to stay in school with the teachers. For me, attending school was not strange, since most of my life, I was always around strange children of diverse groups. I was not a timid child because my parents had encouraged me to participate in religious festivities, which I did. I remember vividly the first poem that I recited in the

Methodist Church. I stood on a bench in order that the audience seated at the back of the church could see my face. That day, I made my parents and Grandma very proud.

I enjoyed attending school, and excelled academically. In our school we had limited materials such as one small black board, and benches were attached to desks and shared by two pupils.

My family referred to me as "Little Poggie," a family nickname for me. As a child, and even as pre-teenager, when my parents referred to me as "Little Poggie" I loved it. However, as I grew older, and started to show interest in the opposite sex, I became embarrassed when they would refer to me as such, and would get very upset with them.

My five years of schooling at "Minerva Public School" were very memorable. I did well both academically and socially. I was awarded a certificate of honor for academic achievement, and got the opportunity to travel along with my teacher to visit the mainland for a week.. I also was awarded a scholarship to attend the teacher training college, "Escuela Normal de Senoritas" for young Ladies in the capital of Tegucigalpa. Yet, like my mother and other females living in my town, I was denied the privilege of accepting the scholarship to pursue my dream of becoming a teacher.

Grandma, as well as some of the people in the community, were strongly against sending their daughters away to school. One of the reasons that Grandma did not allow me to accept, was for fear of the dangers involved in traveling over the rugged terrain, as well as the ongoing attacks on travelers on the highway by the guerrillas. In the beginning of the 1900s, the only means of transportation available was carriages drawn by donkeys. Often the trip between La Ceiba and Tegucigalpa would last for a week if there was no interruptions. Many times the animals would become sick or the caravan would be attacked by the guerrillas, which was most feared than anything else that could happen on the road. It was a risk, yet even living in Coxen Hole, it was possible to be attacked by guerrillas.

My parents would not have been hesitant about my going away to school, but my grandma's constant hammering of the horrible stories about what happened to other people who traveled scared them. My parents felt that if they consented, something bad might happen to me, and it would be nearly impossible to live with it on their consciences. It was possible, but I did not have a chance to go. History repeated itself in our family, and I was the victim, which I regretted. One of my friends and school mate, Francisca Bustillo, was not stopped by her parents in pursing her dream. I was disappointed, and heartbroken the day when I said good bye to my friend Panchita. Most likely Grandma and my parents, especially Chila, did not understand the value of a good education was for either gender. It seemed like Panchita's parents were more aware of what a good education meant. After Panchita's graduation, She taught my older children in P.S. Juan Brooks Elementary.

For sometime, I deeply regretted what I was denied of by Grandma and Chila. Dad understood my feelings, and comprehended my thirst for knowledge. He supported me. Dad tried to explain what was going on, not only in Honduras, but in many of the countries around the world. Some countries were experiencing political changes, others had invasions by military groups. In Honduras, the dreadful and fearful "Black Shirt" guerrilla groups would arrive on the islands unaware, where they would vandalize and terrorize the surrounding communities. All this domestic turmoil made my dad scared for my safety.

As the only girl child at the time, I was always protected by my parents and grandma. As adults, they felt they understood the consequences of the animal-like behavior that these men were capable of exhibiting, especially towards young females. Therefore our parent's fears forced our fathers and brothers to learn how to protect themselves and their families from becoming a victim of these guerrillas by carrying guns. Parents would often spend time teaching the younger males how to use a gun, and would often buy guns for their sons in case they were confronted in the woods. My own brother had a gun, which in the future would cause his death.

At this time in my life, I made a solemn promise to myself and my God, that if He would bless me with a family, I would encourage and support all my children to attain their full potential in life. God later blessed me with many children, and I too experienced similar fears that my parents had been through when it came time for them to leave home to further their education, or to make a living by sailing on the angry billows of the sea. When one is young, it is difficult to understand the life's complexity, but as one gets older and becomes a parent, the whole perspective of life changes.

CHAPTER 4

All the historical events taking place in the mid1800's had spilled over to the early 1900's. This was the result of all the countries in the western hemisphere being under the rule of Spain. They rebelled in pursuit of becoming independent. In 1821, countries from Mexico to Chile were all in a state of rebellion. Years later, on April 21,1861, the Bay Islands were returned to the custody of Honduras. It was a costly price that our ancestors paid for freedom with their blood. These countries had had enough of Spanish slavery, which went on for almost four hundred years during the years of 1492 to 1821.

People lived in daily fear of the mother country, which had the weapons, and was capable of doing anything, including killing her former subjects. Families that resisted often had their parents killed, though the children's lives were often spared. The unharmed families were fortunate if they made their way into the military armory where they were protected, or hide in the mountains or fields.

Our home was just a hundred or more feet away from the armory. Attacks by guerrillas went on for many years until the islands were provided with a larger military force, and better equipment. One day, before these horrible nightmares were over, we were forced to leave our home, and head for shelter. In all our rush, Chila forgot to take her basket that contained her jewelry. Chila was so worried, that one of the soldiers agreed to go by our house and secure the basket.

Another time that I will never forget, was a late afternoon when we were surprised by the guerrillas who did not enter the island from the western end as they usually did. This afternoon, they had landed on the north, as well as the eastern side, and we heard many gun shots in the neighborhood. My parents were in our living room, and I was in my bedroom. My brother was with his friend, when suddenly a bullet came through one of our kitchen windows and went out one of the windows in the living room where my parents were.

I heard Chila screamed my name, she said, "Nana (another nickname of mine) are you laying low, stay low!" I responded to my mother, "Chila, I am staying low." I was so scared. At that moment, I felt Grandma and

Chila's fears that I would be killed by a stray bullet. A few weeks after the incident, our family were in the living room when suddenly we remembered the incident, and started to laugh and joked. Dad imitated Chila by saying, "Nana are you laying low," then Tommy would imitate me, "Chila, I'm laying low." This experience became a family joke for many years after, and it helped to release some of the tension in the atmosphere.

In those days when there was always the appearance of the guerrillas on the islands, people seemed to become more united. Everyone was concerned for each others well being. It seemed as if fear brought people closer together. My family experienced double fear. We feared for the environment, as well as our lives. We especially feared for my father's life. He was well up in age, and his physical health was slowly but surely taking a downward turn. Dad was aware that death was eventually imminent for all, but he felt that his death was nearer. He was going through a silent struggle. He wanted to be with his elderly relatives in Jonesville, yet he wanted to be with us. It was a hard decision he had to make. Daily Dad and Mom talked about what he felt would be best for him. Finally, with a heavy heart dad told us that he had decided not to go back to Jonesville, but requested that if he should die, we should bury him in Jonesville among his deceased relatives. We anticipated dad's death, but little did any one know that our family circle would be broken by the sudden death of Tommy.

On a summer day in 1923, Tommy was cleaning his rifle in the yard under a mango tree, when the gun went off. The bullet hit the neighbor's daughter in the stomach and killed her. When Tommy heard the child screamed, he went towards her lifeless body laying on the ground. He too screamed. Quickly people gathered around, blaming Tommy for being careless with his gun. It was not the first time that my brother had cleaned his gun. He often went hunting along with his friends, but that Wednesday when he was getting ready to go to hunt, tragedy struck. Tommy tried to explain what had happened, but a neighbor yelled that the little girl's father was going to kill Tommy. He still had the gun in his hand, and was shaking like a leaf. I watched the whole scenario from the window. I was shocked when I saw the little girl's body covered with blood. Suddenly, I saw Tommy point the rifle towards his mouth, and pulled the trigger. His body fell to the ground. I screamed, and dad came and took me away. It was horrible sight. By this time, Chila had come from the kitchen and ran out into the yard only to see Tommy's lifeless body on the ground with his face blown off. Chila fell on the lifeless body of her first born, clinging to it and screaming. Dad came out, and struggled with her for her to let go of the body. He then brought her into the house. The news spread quickly in the neighborhood and people came to our yard to see what had happened.

Across the street from our home was the prison, and the soldiers came to the scene. They helped to remove the little girl's body and carried it into her home. They also moved Tommy's body into our home. In the blink of an eye, two people were dead. My brother was a handsome teenager, so full of life with so many dreams for the future, but now all that was gone. Our neighbor's little girl was cut down even before her life had begun. All of these was so painful that I developed an instant headache. I felt like something had hit me on the head, and my head was about to explore.

After the funeral on the following the day at the commentary in the Ticked, I continued to have this headache. It seemed like the medicine I took for the pain was not effective, and the pain went on for days. Parents usually carry a heavy burden when their children die, but I believe it is more painful when the children die tragically. Tommy was young, and had a whole life a head of him. I too experienced the death of three of my own children, but their deaths were not sudden. During their illness, I had hoped that they would recover, and I trusted God to do what was best for them. I claimed God's promise that, "those who hope in the Lord will renew their strength," (Isaiah 40:31). He gave me peace and assurance that one day my dead children and I would be together one glorious day. I believe I will meet my children in heaven. "The Lord kills and makes alive; He brings down to the grave and bring up," (1 Samuel 2:6). Tommy's sudden death left an indelible impression on our family and his friends for some time. Two families mourned the lost of their loved ones. From the day of the accident, our family was shunned by some of our neighbors.

Others neighbors were more sympathetic. They understood that it was an accident, which could have happened to anyone who owned a gun. The little girl's family resented us very much for a while. We earnestly prayed to God that He would give the parents of the little girl emotional strength to bear their loss, and to comfort them. We also indulged in the Word of God in search for comfort. "The Father of mercies and the God of all comfort... Comfort us in all our tribulation, that we may be able to comfort them which are in any trouble by the comfort where with we ourselves are comforted of God," (2 Corinthian 1:3, 4).

His words have been a source of inspiration to help us humans to deal with death. We should not only search His word when we have problems, but feed on it daily to trust Him to give us His peace and assurance that He offers to all.

Prior to Tommy's death, he was in love with a young lady on Goat Hill, living not too far away from him. This young lady was none other than Eva May Allen, and she was pregnant with his child, but he was not aware of this. The young lady kept her pregnancy a secret until the appropriate time when she planned to share the news with Tommy. Unfortunately, his sudden death change everything. A few months later Eva May gave birth on February 26, 1924, to an attractive baby, who was given the name of Judith Veronica Allen.

When Grandma and Chila were told about their future grandchild, their hope was not all lost. At least the child was a part of Tommy, and this brought some comfort to them. As the days and months went by, Chila remained grief stricken over Tommy's death and she looked towards being able to hold and love her grandchild. Dad, Grandma and I were Chila's greatest moral supporters.

Chila blamed herself for allowing Tommy to buy the gun, which he used to end his life. She had plans like most parents had for their children. She planned that Tommy would attend a vocational school in the Capital Tegucigalpa to prepare him to establish his own business someday. She hoped that he would give her some grand children. Unfortunately, he only gave her one lovely granddaughter, whom he never even had the opportunity to meet.

Now Tommy was gone, and Chila's dreams were shattered. To break away from someone we have been bonded to tears apart our emotions. The greater the bond, the greater the pain. It's very painful to face the full impact of our losses, but to adjust to the losses, we have to allow ourselves to feel our pain and ride out the grief. Feeling is healing, and God only has the power to heal the pain.

During the painful times of life, when we have to let go of something or someone dear to us, we find that God is the one to run to. Our family always put God first, despite the situation. Two years later, Dad died, and Chila's lost was greater. She had lost the two men in her life. Dad died very quietly, going to sleep one night. Chila complied with dad's wish to be buried in Jonesville township. Uncle Willie still lived there with his family, wife and two daughters, Elizabeth and Mildred. Uncle Willie was helpful in transporting Dad's body to Jonesville for burial.

After Dad's interment, we spent a few weeks with Uncle Willie and Uncle Henry, who also were advanced in years. They were the two males we looked up to for advice when we needed. We returned back home in Coxen Hole, and resumed our daily lives. The days seemed long and dreary without Dad. Chila continued with her cooking, and Grandma with her sewing, which she did on a very small scale because her eyes were growing dim.

I remembered how our family was when Tommy and Dad were alive. They were always making us laugh around the house, which made the day go by faster. Tommy was a very outgoing young man. He was a very kind and loving person. Dad was a good provider and loving person. On his trips back and forth from the United States of America, Chila, Tommy and I always would receive clothing, perfumes, shoes, sweets, etc.

The lost of my Dad was a very sad occasion. I was aware of course, that having his personal presence with me could not continue indefinitely. But nevertheless, I shall always cherish the things he did that helped me to accomplish my dreams. Dad was a very humorous person. At the same time he was also a stern father.

He always had a smile on his face even when things might not be going well with him. Dad was loved by people both in Coxen Hole, and Jonesville. He was always ready to help and to share what he had with others. Chila was also kind and caring; those attributes made their lives very special. My siblings and I inherited the spirit of sharing from our parents.

My children often complain, that I give away "what I do not have." It is hard for them to understand that we have been able to share with others because of the love we have for other human beings. When Dad died, we came to understand how much the people cared and loved him because of his heart of unselfishness. Our loss was immense, but God gave us the strength to continue with our lives.

Let me take you back to that little attractive daughter of Tommy. Judith as a child was very intelligent and grew up to be a very responsible young lady. I remember the times Judith spent with us. She resembled Chila in many ways; in the color of her skin, body shape and face features. I was a few years older than her, but we got along very well. Judith had a very pleasant attitude, which drew people to her, She also was vibrant, and always smiling. It was a pleasure to have her around, with her strong spirit and character that made her outstanding among her peers.

She was also a very good cook. This was a skill that she inherited from Chila and Grandma.

Judith too had her dream fulfilled. She fell in love with a young man named Jim Welcome, and they got married. They had two daughters whom they named Patricia and Eva Welcome. After some years of family life, Judith and her family migrated to Brooklyn, New York. She continued to bake delicious cakes and breads and cook succulent plates of food. When I ate a piece of Yucca or Coco cake, it reminded me of when I was growing up with Chila. It was remarkable how Chila and I continued to work the cook house. It kept us very busy during the day. We always had new customers. People came from different parts of the world, and continued to visit our island and fell in love with Chila's succulent meals.

Most of the visitors were from Europe. I clearly remember one Italian man of whom rumors spread that he was in search of starting his own business on the Island. This particular gentleman was named Antonio Litrico, and became a regular customer of ours. As time went by, Chila and Antonio developed a close relationship. Chila was a widow, but this did not bother Antonio. They were close in age.

Antonio Litrico was a tall and handsome, wealthy young bachelors from Sicily, Italy. He promised to marry her, but it did not happen. During their relationship, they had two daughters Eloise and America Litrico. It seemed like Chila's destiny was not to get married, but to have relationships and produce children. Nevertheless the results of Chila's relationships were financially and materially positive.

Being an only child for sometime, I had gotten used to all the attention of Chila and Grandma, but I was glad to share with my siblings. I was seven years older than Eloise and eleven years older than America. Despite the gap in our ages, all three of us grew to enjoy each other's company. As my sisters and I grew closer together, something was also happening between Chila and Antonio. He was becoming indifferent and cold towards her, and not too long later the relationship between Chila and Antonio ended.

Chila was still in the prime of her life, and her desire to have another son was part of her ongoing conversation. It wasn't because she didn't love her daughters, but emotionally she was longing for a son to take Tommy's place in her heart. Chila was a dreamer, and had her eyes on a special young man by the name of Joseph Edgar McBride Sr., and they fell in love with each other. Mr. McBride moved in with us. Shortly after my mother fell in love with Joseph, a son, Joseph Edgar McBride, Jr., was born on July 1, 1927, a year and a half before I had my first child.

Chila was independent, financially secure, and more mature than she had been in some of her previous relationships. Her business was still very productive. Edgar soon replaced the place of Tommy in the family.

At this time, my personal life was about to turn into a different direction. Albert and I were dating, and discussing marriage. Grandma McKay was also throwing her hints about when she was going to see her grandchildren. She claimed that she was not very strong, and wanted to at least be able to play with her grandchildren. Some of my friends also were considering marriage and having family.

CHAPTER 5

It had been a long time since Grandma had come to Honduras, and during this time she had fully established herself, but she was advancing in age, and each day her health was getting worse. Yet, she refused to give up her sewing Sewing had been a big part of her life since she had came to Honduras. Grandma wanted to continue sewing clothes for her grandchildren. However, she was eventually forced to stop sewing because the aches and pain in her legs kept her from pedaling the machine. However, she was still able to picture in her mind a dress pattern that she would have like to make for me.

My Grandmother had lived a somewhat comfortable life, and the time came when the vigil began. One day she called for Chila and Willie, and said to them, "I am old, advanced in age, we have seen all that the Lord has done for us." Her words reminded me of the words the Patriarch Abraham when he called for his son Joseph while they were in Egypt. She added that God had been our provider from the onset of our migrating to this country. He has given us more than we deserved. She told Chila and Willing that she was giving all of her earthly possessions to them as an inheritance. She gave Chila the home with most of it's content, and Willie the sewing machine, as well he inherited some of her innate ability to sew. I too learned some of Grandma's sewing skills. I now sew for my children, myself and my neighbors.

While we stood next to Grandma's bed, she added, "keep and make good use of my valuable and precious possessions, because they had been very good to me." Her voice was very strong, and her face glowed, but after that, it was the beginning of the long vigil for some time. Night after night, I stood with Chila beside her bed listening to her breathing as it slowly escape her nostrils, watching the raise and fall of her chest. She remained in the care of the medical practitioner, Dr. Winter, along with the help of caring neighbors and friends. They advised our family, that she could remain in that state for some time. We hoped and prayed to God that He would make good on His promises to answer the prayers of His children.

Chila and I took turn caring for Grandma, while Uncle Willie kept watch over the grandchildren. We often read from Grandma's Bible the numerous promises and passages she had underlined over the years, and we sang her favorite hymns. We wondered if she could hear us. We especially seemed to find comfort in those what had brought special comfort to her heart.

Our waiting was coming to an end. We held Grandma's still hands, and each one of us silently prayed. We stood at her side during that last gloomy morning in late fall in November, 1933. We sang our favorite song, could she hear us? Sometimes it seemed that she could hear, though only her eyes responded. She seemed to especially light up when the names of her grandchildren were mentioned. The final moment finally came for Grandma McKay when she died after a brief illness, along with hypertension which both Chila and I, in our middle age developed. She was 80 years old.

Grandma did not complain, but her facial expressions revealed that all was not right. Chila was like Grandma, when her time came to leave us. She to did not complain about her feelings of pain or discomfort. She remained calm until she died. Both Chila and Grandma were buried in Mount Hole Cemetery, downtown from where we lived. Grandma McKay was mourned by many of her friends; because of the kindness that she had showed to them. It was not common among the residents living in a small community like Coxen Hole to know each other. The community celebrated the birth of each new baby, each wedding, and mourned each death. At the time of Grandma's death, most of the individuals her age had already demised. For most of her life, she had been in good physical, emotional, and most of all spiritual health. For years, she was the matriarch in the circle at the foot of Goat Hill, because of her innate ability to understand others and their needs. Not only did she sew and cook, but she was looked up to for advice about personal issues, as well as home remedies for minor illness such as the common cold or flu, aches and pains.

Some of the advice she often gave to the people who came to her, was that one should always try to talk out their differences, and never to stop; one should never hold grudges against another person. She would then quote a scripture from the Bible such a, "never let the sun go down on your wrath." She strongly believed that people should try to maintain a wholesome relationship with each other.

She also shared receipts of her famous home remedies for colds, which was boiled grape fruit tea sweetened with honey, or ginger and lime with the leaves boiled together. For the fever, especially for children, she would often recommend to wet the head with a mixture of alcohol and ruda (a small green leaves) to help reduce it. These were only some of the ways that Grandma had touched many lives, and that's why it was so hard for us to accept our personal loss. She always said, "God always take the good people first," and "He leaves the bad people to repent from their sins." Now the "good person" in our family had gone to sleep for a while. With the hope that when Jesus return to this earth, I am sure that Grandma will arise from the grave and ascend to heaven with Him. She had a heart of gold.

Grandma saw many changes in her life time. She saw changes in the communication techniques, and the urbanization and suburbanization of Roatan. She lived during the time that the street lights were nothing more than lanterns put on posts. She knew when the government established the first little electric plant to provide electricity to residents from 6:00 p.m. to 10:00 p.m. She also saw the installation of the water system, and the end of the guerrilla's group extinction and the formation of the two major political parties under the names of Democratic (blues) and Republican (reds), and the expansion of the one man road to a much wider one.

I often remember Sunday afternoons, after the midday services, hearing Grandma and some of her contemporaries talk about the changes that were taking place during their life time. By the tone of their voices, I could hear a sense of resentment, but with a flavored of a touch of happiness.

Grandma was also very progressive, like the town she had came to know and loved. She always praised and gave thanks to God for sparing her life so she was able to see so many changes, both in her family life and her environment. She not only was able to experience being a grandmother, but also a great grandmother and aunt.

Grandma was not an ordinary woman, she was an exceptional woman; a one-of-her-kind among her peers. She often used the statement that she was born with wisdom, and she was going to die with understanding. To describe Grandma McKay accurately, I lack the appropriate words, but what I can proudly say about this remarkable woman, is that she had made a difference in the lives of many families during the years that the Good Lord Blessed her with.

My grandmother was a woman who loved her family and walked humbly with Her God. She spent her life working hard at her sewing and cooking business. She always acted justly with her neighbors. She was merciful to all. She walked the walk that God calls us to. Her whole life was an example for Chila, and her three daughters to carry on all that Grandma had initiated. "The Little Cook House" grew to a famous "Cook House." on the top of Goat Hill.

Grandma was gone, and only Uncle Willie remained alive from the small company of three brave and courageous individuals who sailed from their native land Belize to the unknown country of Honduras. Uncle Willie lived a few years after his mother died. He too did not lay in bed any length of time before he was called to rest by our God. He was buried in the town of Jonesville next to my father and his uncle. He left his wife and children which mourned his death. Chila and I maintained contact with the rest of our relatives, and as the years went by, they too died, leaving a new generation of one-hundred-percent Hondurans.

CHAPTER 6

Growing up on the island had it's good and bad moments. One of our customs was Saturday afternoon picnics on the beach. Families would pack baskets with food and drink, and head for the beach on the rock islet, which was only two hundred or so feet from the big island. We crossed the sea either by canoe or sometimes we would swim. Swimming was one of my favorite sports. I would often swim with some of my friends. We enjoyed swimming, and we were very good at it. We did not have any Olympic games, because my team would have won every gold medal. The girls competed against the boys. We girls had a very strong team of swimmers, composed by our leader, Myra, Thelma (her sister), Luella, Colita, Sylvia, Castella and myself. We swam like fish in the sea, and we were very fast swimmers.

One Saturday evening, our team met at the foot of the wharf, ready to plunge into the sea and head toward the key from the big island. We were only half way towards the key when we herd voices yelling at us from the wharf, trying to get our attention. When we looked back, we saw some men beckoning us to return to shore. We were advised to return, because the water just off the key was infested with sharks We got scared and turned around, swimming towards the wharf as fast as we could. When we arrived, we were out of breath, but glad to be out of those waters, and that someone was kind enough to advise us of the danger.

Later on we were informed that deep in the bottom of the sea, was a buried pirate ship between the island and the key called "The Snig." The ship had sunken hundreds of years ago. The fishermen told stories about large sharks that lived many hundred miles below, and how the sharks had the tendency to come to the surface to look for food, especially when the other ships disposed of their garbage. Despite all that we had heard, we were a daring group of girls, willing to risk our lives to show off our bodies and our skills at swimming. For a few days we stayed away from swimming, but shortly we resumed our recreation activities.

We wanted the attention of the opposite sex. Young people then were no different from young folks of today. We enjoyed coquetting, teasing and showing off our bodies, but that was as far as it went, because if any one of us got fresh. Any adult was at liberty to reprimand a young girl or boy if they were seen doing anything they considered to be out of the norm. If an adult spoke to one of us, you just stood there without answering back, and without a frown on your face.

Today things have definitely changed. I recently had an experience with a five-year-old boy, who was pulling on my fence. I told him kindly to stop pulling at my fence. The words that came out of his mouth were unbelievable. As a young child or a teenager, we were not allowed to go on the street alone or to go to any gathering without a chaperon. These chaperons may be a parent or a neighbor. Today, teenagers often travel to distant lands in groups without any adult supervision. This was never heard of when I was a young girl, or even as I reared my own children with the same discipline I was accustomed to as a child.

Another memorable experience I remember, was one of the Saturday Night dances held in the Municipal Building or at the Free Mason Building. Usually these nights were magnificent displays of young ladies wearing elegant gowns, which showed the contour of the ladies bodies; the girls felt like queens. I was one of the two shorter ones at five feet, one inch. I cruised across the dance floor, holding on to Albert's arm (my secret admirer), a gentleman who was six feet, one inch. Some Saturday nights the dances fell on Christmas Eve. It was customary for us to go to the midnight mass held in the church. We left for the dance hall then left the dance hall to attend church for mass and then returned to the dance. We stayed until sunrise on Christmas day. Then we would take cake and other goodies to the elderly, sick or shut in. We later attended the parade of clowns which culminated with games, plat pole, and grease pole, and various native dances. Most young ladies had a very high level of energy and tolerance, especially when one felt like they were on top of the world, and one was able to do a lot of things at the some time. I am happy that I can now sit and reminiscence on the past.

There are two other memorable moments, I wish to share. I loved to take care of our flowers garden and watch butterflies flying from flower to flower. On one of my father's trips to the United States, he brought home rose buds of almost every color. We planted a flower garden. In our garden we grew red, yellow, white, and pink roses, gardenias, rooster comb, sun flowers, violets, orchids, etc. I spent many late evenings in the garden. I was surrounded by the flowers and roses, which brought a deep sense of tranquility to my being. I often thought about Adam and Eve in the beautiful garden of Eden, and how thrilling an experience it must have been to smell the different fragrances of the flowers; to see them bloom into natural beauty that only God could create. Most likely Adam and Eve spent a lot of time smelling flowers in the Garden, as I did at night, as I patiently waited for the orange trees to extricate their pleasant fragrance. I planted a night bloom tree in the front yard, just after Albert and I moved into his father's home. The tree was planted next to the gate facing the main street. The night bloom tree served two purposes, aesthetics, and as a means to discipline my children and later on my grandchildren. My children and grandchildren will attest to the many times when I used branches from that tree on their buttocks to punish them. The little tree withstood many hurricanes in it its life time dating back to the 1930s.

My friends always asked permission to cut a limb from this tree, so they could plant in their yards. Unfortunately none of them were successful in growing the plant. Sometimes, I felt that the plant resented being taken apart. I even attempted to have the plant grow roots in a pot for one of my friends, but I did not succeed. The plant seemed to refuse to take root easily.

On my 17th birthday, Chila had a surprise birthday party for me on June 24, 1925. She invited some of my friends whom she thought merited the honor to attend. She prepared the food, played music on the victrola. Chila wanted to display her grown attractive young lady to the gentlemen. She was proud of her "Little Poggie," who had grown into a very beautiful woman, and she did not hide her feelings in describing me to friends. I was aware at the time some of my friend's mothers did not feel comfortable with Chila praising me before them. I knew deep down in Chila's heart that she did not want to make anyone feel bad, but she was proud to have a daughter and at the same time most likely she was hoping for me to find a young man whose attention I would catch. Little did she know that had already happened, unaware to her. I had my eye on Albert, and he had his eye secretly on me.

Albert was one of the young men that had watched us while we engaged in any gathering weather at church, weddings, school, or swimming on Saturdays. He especially had singled me out among my friends. Often we would catch a glance at each other, and it was a thrill for both of us. Albert and I also would share little notes by one of his male friends. These brief eye contacts, and little note sharing was exciting, since no one was allowed to date without their parent's permission or approval. Now Chila was having my birthday party, and Albert had been one of those invited. We spent a very pleasant evening together, something to remember for a long time. For days I felt like I owned the universe. Whenever I remembered the way my friends had admired me, I got a good feeling, but whenever I thought about Albert, the feeling was totally different than any feeling I had ever experienced. That was the feeling of love. I surely loved that feeling, and I was praying that one day God would bring us together. I had other admirers, from a distant as well, but deep inside of me I knew this one was different.

Sometime we girls would get together and dream about our wedding day and children. In those days, parents all looked forward to their children, especially their daughters getting married, and they were encouraged to do so, and the daughters too were looking to find the man of her dream. Years later my dream became a reality.

CHAPTER 7

Chila was instrumental in bringing Albert and I together. She confessed that she was not aware that by inviting this handsome guy to my surprised birthday party, one day he would become her son-in-law, and the progenitor of the "Connor Clan."

Albert Eduardo Connor was 27 years old. He was tall, quiet and skinny. He was the man who later became my husband. Albert and I were attracted to each other from early on. Grandma and Chila seemed to like the match, and they gave us permission to date, but with their supervision. Finally after two years of dating, Albert found enough courage to ask Chila for my hand in marriage, and Chila agreed, but with some reservation. She wanted to make sure that I would not have the same experience as she had.

At the same time, Chila's business was still going strong, and she needed all the additional hands to help her in the kitchen. I too agreed with Chila. Her fears and concerns for her business were natural. But I wanted what seemed best for me.

I was 20 years old, and deeply in love with Albert who was now 26 years old. He was the man of my dream. During our courtship, I always fantasied about life with Albert. He was loving and kind, serious about life, and it seemed he had the ability to be successful at whatever he did. Albert was skillful. He played the guitar, clarinet and mandolin. He was also a master barber like his father. Albert spent most of his free time at his father's barber shop. When he was still quite young, he began trying his barber skills on his friends in his backyard. At age 18, he became a partner with his father. Next he opened Albert's Barber Shop. Albert was a true master "Barber," who was well known throughout the islands.

Chila and Grandma thought that Albert was not exciting, but mature; they thought him to be boring. As parents they had hoped that I would fall in love with a business man or a sailor like my father. They had judged Albert wrongly. One had to spend time with Albert to get to know him, and I did.

Albert was no saint, but he was a lot of fun. He had a sense of humor and was enthusiastic about his work, but he was also conservative like grandma. Albert and I planned secretly to consolidate our relationship, and then we informed Chila. We were aware of the risk of starting a family, but we were willing to take that risk.

Albert was the son of Terrell Varrell Connor III and Susanna Lucas. According to him, his great grand parents were immigrants, who during the years of 1845–1849 had immigrated from the providence of Kerry, Ireland to the Cayman Island, and then to the Bay Island of Honduras. At this time, Ireland was going through political and religious changes. The English Parliament conquered Ireland, and confiscated the whole of the country from the legal owner. These changes mostly likely had some influence on Albert's relatives in leaving Ireland, along with those who the English government sent to other countries as indentured laborers. In addition, Albert's great-grandfather, Terrell Varrell O'Connor, had been disinherited by his father in Ireland because he had choose to marry the daughter of one of the miners. She belonged to a lower socioeconomic class than his father. As a result, Terrell was told that he no longer belonged to the O'Connor family. Terrell accepted his parents decision, and he rebelled by not carrying the family surname, so he dropped the letter "O" from his name, and his name became Terrell Connor.

Terrell looked for a way to escape from his father's anger. He and his wife Maryann left Ireland on a vessel bound for Cayman Island, where they started a new life. They had three children: Rycroft, Clotilde and Terrell II, who later married Susana. He and his siblings grew to adults, they all got married and had a family of their own. Terrell II and Susanna had three children together called Henrietta, Livingston, and Albert. Albert was born in Roatan on July 21, 1901. Three years after Albert's birth, his mother died, leaving his father to raise young Albert and his older siblings with some help from his aunt Clotilde Tetum-Connor.

Albert's father was a master barber who was well known through the island. He taught his two boys the skill of barbering, but Albert was the only one that learned the craft, and soon gained a following of his own customers and made it his career. Albert's brother, Livingston, left home at age seventeen. He joined the Merchant Marines. He sail from Puerto Cortes to different countries in the world. Later on, Livingston made Puerto Cortes his home.

His older sister Lucy got married to Lionel Patterson from up the Mosquito Coast. They had a large family, and moved to live in La Ceiba. Albert's younger siblings married, Henrietta to Castulo Rivera, who was much older than she. She got married before Albert. Her father was not in agreement with the gentleman whom she married to, and he was very upset, that he publicly disowned her. Relatives and friend attempted to persuade Terrell to change his mind and attitude towards his daughter choice of husband. Henrietta's husband had many marital problems from the onset of their relationships. Their marriage did not last long. She was deserted by her husband, for another woman close to his age, and rejected by her father.

Albert was the only one she could turned to, but he was not in any financial position to help with her plan. Henrietta's plan was to migrate to the island of Cuba, which at that time was in its bloom. It was one of the most attractive places in the Caribbean, and this description was soon widely known. People frequently moved from Honduras to Cuba, and vice verse. Henrietta never returned to Honduras, neither did she made any attempt to communicate with her family. The first and last information on Henrietta came from her brother Livingston during one of his trips from Honduras to the United State. His ship ran into a storm, and was forced to deviate from the regular route and landed off the Cuba's coast and was taken ashore. There Livingston made a sad discovery. He discovered that his sister Henrietta's body was laid in a funeral parlor across from a bar where he and his friends were having a few drinks. He was informed by a fellow crew member from another vessel who had been walking around the vicinity earlier in the story. His friend had been approached by a stranger, who asked him where he was from. The stranger asked him if he knew a lady by the name of Henrietta Connor, originally from Honduras. When Livingston learned of his sister death, he immediately left the bar with the intention to go to the funeral home. He got there and found that the corpse in the coffin resembled his sister. The funeral director told Livingston that he knew his sister for many years. Unfortunately, Terrell Connor never got to know about his daughter because he died in 1941.

My reason to include the Terrell O'Connor's story is to show that some previous family experiences repeat themselves. I believe that no family is exempted from a feud, no matter where the family lives on this earth. Compared with my family, Albert's family appears to have had more bickering than mine. I had hoped and prayed that when we became parents, and our children grew up and decided to have families of their own, Albert and I would do our best to go along with their choice of a life's partner, if it did not conflict with God's principles. But with Albert being the kind of person he was, I was not too sure. Albert was not a person to really express his feelings openly, and I was convinced that it would be difficult for him to do so, but I would. I have learned that sometimes it is best not to be too open with our feelings towards our children.

My Heavenly Father in His glorious way brought two young people together, and after sometime our relationship, like most courtships, one would expect for it to end up in marriage.

On November 28, 1928, Our marriage became a reality a the Zion Methodist Church. Reverend Fred McNeil "tied" us together with cords of love. It was on a rainy Saturday afternoon that our dream became reality in the presence of family, and friends. Those cords could not be seen, but they lasted for 32 years. I call it God's providence, because we had procreated a houseful of children.

During the first years of our marriage, Albert and I lived in Grandma's house at the foot of Goat Hill, in front of his barber shop. Three of our children were born in this house before we moved to another house, and finally to Albert's father house to live, in the Ticket, to help take care of his ailing father. In this house four of our children were born. Albert and I and the children lived in this house for 32 years, until six years after Albert's death, when it began falling down upon us.

CHAPTER 8

Our marriage was not without a price. We had our good times, and those times which were not as good. However, our family gave us support, and we thank God for His blessings that were poured upon our family. Albert and I agreed not to get discouraged when the hard times came. Family will be family, and at times Chila and Grandma attempted to interfere with Albert and I, when they assumed that all was not well. One day I was talking to Chila, and she revealed that she was really happy for me, because I did what she did not do. She congratulated me for making my own family while she was alive. She also confessed that she realized that she was putting her own needs before my needs.

For thirty two years, Albert and I shared our lives together. The transition from living alone to living with another person was a challenge. Furthermore, nurturing and caring for nine children and having financial problems was a great experience. With the good Lord's help to our family, we realized that our children were a blessing. The Psalmist David said in the Bible, "blessed is the man that has a quiver of them." Paul also states in the Book of Corinthians that, "children are a treasure." In my opinion, children are wonderful treasures that extend blessings to other people.

Albert and I became parents shortly after our marriage. Between May 29,1929 and May 27, 1953, we had four boys and six girls. All of our children came into this world by natural birth. We could not afford to do it any other way. I thank God that I did not had any complications during pregnancy. Their weight ranged from nine pounds to eleven pounds. Dr. Policarpo Galindo and the midwife Mrs. Tinny Woods, who was a very gentle and caring person, helped with their deliveries.

Albert and I agreed to named our children in chronological order. There names are Tomas Woodrow, Eduardo Albert (Wavi), Armando Sirr (Mandingo deceased) Olimpia Zetella (Pimpa), Ruperta Angela (Perta); Elvia Ercilia (Blackey-deceased) Susana America, (Sue) Guillermina Eloisa (Mina), Margarita Rose (deceased) and Terrell Varrell Connor. The Connor's household took a period of 24 years to come into being. We give God praise and thanks for every one of our children. Raising a family, was an educational experience for us. In our family we could not show favoritism. We learned to love each child equally, despite their individual differences. We realized that each one of our children was unique. Each child had the ability to love, to care, to create, and to grow, and we instilled in each other that God loves each one as if they were the only one in the world. In addition, we taught our children self respect and respect for all. Our children did their best not to be rebellious when they were told about the rules of our home. I guess it's only natural for children to attempt to get their parents attention by one means or the other such as fighting among themselves, crying or even having temper tantrum. Throughout the hectic times, I prayed to God to help keep me calm and in control of the situation. This was very challenging, but we were aware that God was watching over us and all things were going to workout well.

Our family was interrupted by the cold of hands of death for the first time in 1950 when our dear and precious child Margarita Rose died in La Ceiba. This was my most difficult pregnancy. The family doctor advised Albert and I to seek medical attention on the mainland, where they had more medical services to offer.

Albert and I, along with my two younger daughters, traveled to La Ceiba, and we stayed at Lolo's house, next to the Seventh-day Adventist Church. It was good advice, because my life was saved, but unfortunately my baby did not live. She was born with a blood disease, and had a very low red cell count. Her anemia ultimately cost her her life.

On April 5th, I had gone into labor and shortly, I gave birth to a doll-like baby. For five days, God blessed us to be able to see our baby alive. He gave us the chance to hold her fragile little body in our arms, to stare into the perfect features of our little girl engraving them in our mind, to feel the warmth of her ailing body next to mine. Day and night everything that was humanly and medically possible was done to correct the course of Margarita's illness, but as I held her each day, I felt the warmth go out of the little body, yet I still could not give her up.

Finally, on April 10, 1950, in the evening Margarita's heart stopped. She was next to the last girl child. I called for my two younger girls. Their little sister would never grow up to be their friend, and this broke my heart to see the look on their faces as well as my husband's face. My tears just flowed, and I thought they would never stop. It was not easy for us to listen to Margarita's mourning, but while she mourned, there was life. It was more painful to see her little body laying still in her coffin in the church, but it was encouraging to know that one day we would see her again on that day of resurrection, when God will give her back to us.

Our precious baby was now a harmless, defenseless little body that would be destroyed. Margarita's body returned to the earth. The Lord stood by our side, and gave us the strength which we needed to confront the days ahead. It was a traumatic experience for us.

My homecoming was not one of victory, but desperation for the rest of the family friends who was hoping to see our baby. My healing resulted from my husband's understanding of what I had been through, which was more painful for me than for himself. I was also confronted by the the closeness of the rest of family members and the well wishes of friends. After all, I was the one who felt the kicking in my womb and heard the heartbeat for nine month After some time, life returned to what would be normal. But even after all these years, not a day passes that I do not think of my Margarita's death. I felt an emptiness in my heart, knowing that I would never hold Margarita's body next to mine, to nurse her, or to caress her soft skin, and I would never see her grow up or hear her laughter like the way I enjoyed with my other children. Years later, this pain was added to with the deaths of my husband, two adult children, and Chila. There is an emptiness deep inside that would never be filled. Oh, how I longed for the resurrection day when I would see them again.

As I remember these dear loved ones of mine, I wonder how God's heart must break over the eternal loss of every man, woman, and child. He too must have the feelings of emptiness deep inside Him, feelings which will never be filled either. Death is cruel. It was difficult for me to deal with, but I came to grip with myself that our Heavenly Father is our ruler and creator, and we must submit to His will. He knew what my baby's future would be like, and prevented our family from going through it. Maybe her future would be one of prolonged suffering for herself and her family. Now I can say with hope, whatever path God chooses for us, whatever way He ordains for our lives, that is the only path of safety.

I would like to go back to the years of the Great Depression, when our older children were still very young. The Great depression began in 1929. It affected the whole world. We had three active boys to provide for. Albert's barber and shoemaker business was very slow at this time. Apparently people were not spending their money, or they did not have any to spend. In some cases, even if there was money there was little food to buy. Most of the families on the island resorted to growing their own food. Fishing was very important in order to provide food for their families. Families often exchanged produce or fish with each other, or in exchange for labor. God blessed us so we did not have to go to bed without food.

Before the depression was over, two more daughters were born. In the late 1938, business on the island was starting to get better, but another worldwide phenomenon had developed, World War I, bringing fear into our hearts. Our husbands, sons, and uncles were all enlisted to go to war. Albert enlisted, but he did not go to war. It might have been that Albert was a coward. He was fearful for his life, and Albert later confessed to me that he never had any desire to travel abroad, and he could not see himself firing a gun at another human being, or living daily with the uncertainty about his life. I agreed with him. I did not want to be separated from Albert either, nor did I want to care for our children alone. Our plan was to live together until old age.

Albert, was the kind of individual that preferred to be with his family. He was aware that people were dying in order to bring peace in the world, but his inner feelings were strong and he believed in self preservation. Albert joked that he would stay behind to defend the island, and to keep things moving until the other men returned from the war. In the future, Albert traveled because of his illness to seek medical attention elsewhere in a few neighboring countries such as Belize and Guatemala.

CHAPTER 9

On the eve of World War I, our eldest son Tomas began attending elementary school at Juan Broks Public School. As parents we spent a lot of time to prepare him for the transition from home to school environment. Tomas was anxious to attend school, but we were more anxious than he. We wonder how he would adjust. I had thought that we had prepare ourselves for the years when our children would attend school, but as each one of them reached school age our anxiety was less. Albert, for the first days of Tomas' school attendance, he would inquire but as the time when by he took it slightly. I realized that my full time job of mothering, was weaving away. I would be losing a big chunk of my favorite job of caring for our children and realized that I had to do something or make a change to hold on to my favorite role.

In order for me to be in close contact with the school environment, I joined the Parent Teacher Association (PTA). In the second school year, I was voted in as president of the PTA. I wanted to be an integrate part of my son's education, and I strongly believe in the power of education. As I had been deprived of my dream of becoming a teacher, I promised myself, that if God ever blessed me with children, I would do all that was humanly possible for my children to acquire an education. I held the position president from 1938-1940s, and continued as active participant until our youngest daughter entered school. The only public school in Coxen Hole still exists as I write. A few private schools have now open up there, along with few other secondary schools. God has blessed our family, that all of my children attended the same elementary school and graduated, except for Eduardo who only attended school up to third grade. Eduardo had some developmental delays. Most of our other children attended the secondary education level in various institutions in Honduras, such as in Roatan, La Ceiba, San Francisco Atlantida and Tegucigalpa.

Performing the various roles in life as a mother, wife, homemaker and president of the PTA, was tiresome, but I enjoyed ever moment of it. Even though I got so tired from the daily chores that I felt like not attending the PTA meetings held twice per month, I convinced myself that I had to be there since I had made the commitment. In addition, I actively participated in social affairs of the Methodist Church to make sure my children were exposed to spiritual things. I also was a member of the only female club, "Merry Bee." This club met once per week on Thursday afternoons, in one of the member's home, and we usually served refreshment. It served many purposes as an outlet for our bundled up feelings, about raising a family, and many other topics. To our amazement, we shared similar problems which are common in most families, and we were able to provide each other with some means of solution, or we would just have sharing time and general conversation, followed by planning some future activities for the group.

This group was formed by some single and married females, most of us were also childhood friends. Their names are as follows: Thelma and Myra S. (sisters-deceased), Luella T, Olive T, Francisca (deceased), and Lucila B, Minnie and Almighty E (relatives), Marie G, Aifreda B, Sylvia M, Esmeralda P, Colita J and myself. Our club remained in existence for many years, until members began to migrate to other parts of the country and to foreign countries especially to the United State of America. These members participated when they were on vacation in the island, but the few of us that remained did not feel the same enthusiasm as when all the members were there.

Our main task was to plan and organize school plays, and civic activities like Independence Day (15 of September) and carnival celebrations or fund-raising for special projects. We competed with other teams in volleyball in French Harbor, Jonesville and Oak Ridge, and teams from the Islands of Utila and Guanaja. The member's biggest hurdle was over, our children were growing up, the need to remain together did not seemed to be as great. Finally, in the middle of 1959, we held our last meeting with seven or eight members that still remained on the island. We sang our team song "We the Merry Bee" for the last time, and cried and laughed, reminiscing on the "good old days" that we had spent together. At that time, I felt like part of me had died. I believed it was a mutual feelings among the ladies. Thursday afternoons were not the same without the "Merry Bee" club meetings. But we were able to maintain contact with each other through the church. All good things have an end, and the club broke up. Currently, only two of the members from the club are still alive [As of 1996] Lucila B and myself. As far as I can remember, there has never been another female club organized in Coxen Hole like the "Merry Bee."

During the 1950s, I had witnessed two deaths: the first was my daughter Margarita in La Ceiba and the second was the death of the "Merry Bee" club. Both deaths were painful because there was a permanent absence. Human beings need to be in contact with each other in order for us to grow. The club had served as means of personal and social growth, but every good thing always come to an end; that is the law of nature. We are made with the innate capacity to remember both the happy and unhappy moments in our lives. These memories of the time our club members shared together cannot be easily forgotten. Our lives had to go on. So we pick up the pieces, and we moved on with hope for very best. Before WW II was over on December 31,1946, we had two daughters added to our family. Three of our children: Armando, Olimpia, and Ruperta attended elementary school, and our oldest son was one year away from completing his studies at the "Bellas Artes" Vocational School. I was about to see one of my dreams come true. Albert and I were grateful to God for His blessing upon our son. We were proud because my children were moving in the right direction in terms of their education. In addition, our family was happy too, because Eloise and Antonio Crimmings got married after America and Steve Trusty a few years later. Both my sisters moved to the mainland, to the city of La Ceiba, Atlantida for some time. Eloise and Antonio, did not have children of their own but they adopted a baby boy, whom they named Antonio Crimmings Jr.

Antonio Crimmings Sr. was originally from West End Town of the island. His parents were Johanna and George Crimmings, and he had two sister Ira and Eileen. He was a merchant marine. In the Mid 1950's, Antonio (Tony) and Eloise (Lolo) migrated to the United states, where they settled down in New Orleans, Louisiana. They traveled frequently back and forth to visit the family in Honduras. They did this for many years.

Unfortunately, in mid 1960's, Lolo and Tony experienced one of the most challenging and painful moments in their lives. Their only child in his late teens, had kept the wrong company, and was on the wrong side of the "River Louisiana" at the wrong time, was alleged to be involved with the shooting of a white police officer. He was tried, and sentenced to be in prison for over thirty years.

Tony Jr., is a very strong headed man. He often got involved in fights with other inmates. This contributed him not being able to appeal before the Board of Parole. While Tony remained in prison, both parents died without seeing him a free man. Antonio died in July 1982, in Roatan and

Eloise died on February 13, 1988, in New Orleans. Tony's prison social worker was informed about his mother's death, and she made arrangement to obtain a permission for him to attend his mother's funeral. He was brought to the funeral parlor to see his mother's corpse under heavy security for an hour, and then he was returned to prison.

On the day of Lolo's funeral, it was the first time I was going to see Tony Jr., since he left Honduras in the fifites. I was heart broken when I saw my nephew all bonded in chains around his feet and waist. My first thought was to go over and embrace him, but I restrained my self from doing so, and silently sent a prayer up to our Heavenly Father on his behalf. Lolo also helped raise two of America's older children Emilio and Zulma. They were from America's previous marriage. America my younger sister met Steven Trusty and they got married, and from that union four additional children were born: One pair of twins Steve and Cristina, and another set of fraternal twins Rudy and Rupert Trusty. Years later America and Steven separated.

America worked in one of the city hospitals in La Ceiba as a nurse's aide. She struggled to raise her four children alone. In the late 1950s, America moved with her children to the second largest city in Honduras, San Pedro Sula. She not only found work, she also found a husband by the name of Jose Louis Castillo. They did not have any children together, so they adopted a baby girl, and named her Lillian Leticia Castillo.

America and her family lived in San Pedro Sula for many years. Before her two eldest children Emilio and Zulma, were sponsored by Lolo to go to New Orleans to attend school. She and the rest of family members eventually moved to New Orleans in the 1960s. It was not difficult for America to find employment in the Tauro Hospital located in her neighborhood, where she worked for many years. America and Jose ended their marriage after several years, and she remained single for awhile until Cupid's arrow pierced America's heart again, and soon wedding bells rang in the air for America and Peter Moret, who was a much older man than she was. Peter died a few years later, and America retired from her job. Tragedy struck her health. She had a stroke, followed by several mini ones, which forced her to stay in the hospital. Slowly America's health deteriorated to the point where she depended on a cane to assist her in walking. She still resides in New Orleans with her children and grandchildren.

America and I always maintained a good relationship. We gave birth one after the other, from 1940-1946, when she stopped, yet I continued and gave birth to two more children. We practiced the good old "hand-me-down" rule between our children. Our children's clothing and shoes traveled back and forth from one house to the other house for many years. As we grew older, we often reflected on how we raised our children, how we exchanged clothing and so on. It is possible that America and I were very close because of the many children we had. America and I had our children in the same order as Chila. Our brother Joseph also got along well. On the other hand, the relationship between Lolo and myself was not that great, but we got along somewhat superficially.

Joseph Edgar McBride Jr., was Chila's last child. As mentioned, Chila's first child was a boy, and her last also was a boy. At times I felt like Joseph was my own child. Edgar or Junior, my brother as he was called by family and friend, was only a year older than my oldest son. As a child he was very active. He did everything in a hurry. He did not lose anytime coming into this world, he broke many young lady's hearts, and he got married at an early age and started a family before the rest of his siblings. Junior was what they called in Honduras a "Don Juan." He finally stopped his wild life when he met and fell in love with a young woman by the named of Doris Bodden, and a short time later, they got married.

This young lady was from the township of Flowers Bay, eight miles from Coxen Hole, the same town where Chila was born. Junior and his wife, Doris Bodden, lived in Coxen Hole for sometime. He was a butcher. They later moved to the mainland like his two sisters. Chila and I were the only ones from my family that lived on the island. Doris and Junior had seven children: Alonzo, Valda, Joel, Norvil, Gilbert, Doris, and Marco Antonio McBride. He always traveled from one town to the other in search of cattle. Junior was a friendly person. As a result of Junior's gregarious behavior, he had an argument in 1963 with one of his friends, and they shot each other. Junior's injury was not fatal, unfortunately his friend's was. After weeks of hospitalization Junior's friend died. He was tried, but was released based on the argument that he acted in self defense. Junior's friend's family did not accepted the judge's sentence, and they tried to take his life. Junior was blessed by God, who was watching over him and his family.

In March 1963, Junior and his household returned to the island for some time, and later they escaped to Belize because the family of his dead friend, determining to find him and take their revenge, or on any of his relatives. This had us all very scared for our own safety for some time. In order for us to have a peace of mind, Junior and family took a vessel to Belize in October 1966.

Our family back on the island did not hear from Junior for many years. The first time we heard from Junior was in the end of 1966, a friend of the family who resided in Belize brought word from Junior, that all was well with him and his family. After 1966, we heard from Junior regularly. He was afraid to write for fear of being tracked down by his pursuers, and he wanted to protect the rest of family in Roatan. Because of the uncertainty from day to day that surrounded Junior's life, Chila worried immensely about her baby. She would always inquire with people that traveled to Belize if they saw him. She had hopes that one day Junior would return home on a visit or to stay. She yearned to see her child and to talk to him, but Chila never had the privilege to see him again. She died three years later after we first heard from him on March 28, 1969.

Currently, no one knows whether or not Junior is alive. Sometime ago in the 1970s, we got news from Belize that Junior's wife Doris had died. We got the news from a lady who had traveled to that country. Junior had some similarity to Chila, Tommy, and grandma McKay. He was the only one of Chila's children who married someone from her home town Flowers Bay, where Chila was born. Unfortunately, Junior, like Tommy, shared a similar fate because of their love for arms. As stated before, Tommy accidentally shot another person. Finally, Junior migrated to Belize, the country where Grandma originally came from to Honduras.

In 1993, my second son Wavi received an unexpected visit from a young man who claimed to be Junior's son Alonzo. He inquired about me. My son stated that Alonzo was in a hurry to take the airplane back to Belize, so they did not get a chance to talk as they wished. That was the last time I heard anything about Junior. I had not given up hope, to see Junior and his family. I often pray to God for him and his family's safety, and I would often mail a card to his last known address. This story will continue exclusively with events in the life of the Connor-Andrew family.

CHAPTER 10

Our family was doing well by the 1950s. We had three income from the boys, along with Albert's, made us comfortable, even though we were owing money due to Albert's sickness. For many years, Albert had suffered from ulcerated stomach. He was treated, and improved for awhile. In the latter part of the 1950s, Albert's sickness worsened, which I believe was attributed to stress and his increased drinking habit.

Albert hemorrhaged in his stomach, and required immediate medical attention. He was taken to see the doctors on the mainland, but he did not completely improve, so he traveled to Belize, and ended up in Puerto Barrios City Hospital in Guatemala. The treatment he received was helpful. Albert returned home and continued to improve. He eventually was able to return to work, and our family's life return to normal.

Our children continued with their education and older ones worked. In November of 1957, it was an exciting moment when I heard over the radio the graduation ceremony of our oldest daughter from teacher school, "Normal de Senoritas" in Tegucigalpa, where she had been attending for the past five years. Our second daughter was working as an assistant teacher in the rural area. She also was taking correspondence courses toward becoming a teacher. Everything went well with our family until one day when I learned that Albert was having an extra-marital affair with a lady that I knew.

It was a beautiful, quiet, night. The moon was full, and shining bright, and a friend of Albert's and mine came to my home, and encouraged me to take a walk with her uptown. My friend was aware of Albert's relationship with the sister of her neighbor. She had seen them together frequently, and decided that it was time for me to know what was going on. I agreed that I would walk uptown as soon as my children were gone to bed. It was about 7:30 p.m. when we left the house, and shortly, we got to the park and to my surprise, I saw Albert sitting in the park between two sisters with his hand embracing one. I yelled at Albert. I questioned how could he be cheating on me. He did not respond, and I walked up to him and slapped him on the cheek. The lady that sat next to Albert said to me "Albert and I are only friends." I told her that he was embracing her. My friend and I then continued on our stroll.

Later on when I returned home, I found Albert fast asleep in his bed. The next day Albert did not say anything to me about the incident in the park, but guilt was written all over his face. I told Albert that he had failed to keep our marriage vows. I told him that he was unfaithful to me and what he was doing was not right in the sight of God. Albert did not respond. His silence made me angry. I yelled at him, that I have been intimately involved with only one man and he was that man. I still did get an answer.

Albert ate his breakfast that day, and left for his barber shop. Albert did not enjoy keeping malice, so he made peace with me. Maybe Albert got a grip on himself when he realized, what he was doing to our marriage. He stated that he strongly loved his family, and he is a good provider. He also stated that he realized that we had been married for twenty years plus and never cheated on each other. I had many opportunities to get involved with another man but I did not do so. Albert's barber shop was only about ten feet away from where we lived, and it was trafficked by men all day long. Some of Albert's customer attempted to make sexually innuendo towards me, but I knew better to even considered any type of flirtation.

At this time in our lives, we should have been centered around our family and not on extra-marital affairs. What made this incident so embarrassing was that our older children were grown and Albert was behaving like one of them. I too had to reflect on my aggressive behavior, and set an example for our children.

Shortly, after this incident towards the end of 1952, I got pregnant with my last child. I had secret plans for this child to enter the ministry. I used to think about him as my little Samuel. I made a promised to God, that I was going to dedicate my son to Him. This child was the only one of our children that attended an Adventist College in Pena Blanca, San Pedro Sula, so that he would have a different education experience. Despite of all the effort and sacrifice of the family provided, it did not happened. He had a mind of his own. By God mercy and grace, I set the right example for all of my children to follow even before I came to know Three Angels' Message.

On May 29, 1953, I was a middle aged woman facing mid-life crisis, when I gave birth to a 11 pounds child, whom I named Terrell Varrell. His weight was three pounds heavier than any other child I had before.

After I gave birth, I started to have some difficulty with my health. I struggled with terrible headaches and dizziness and blackout. I had my last period before my last pregnancy, and I thought everything was well. But things changed. I went to see the family doctor. He told me that I was entering menopause, and my childbearing years was over.

I was 45 years old, and scared because of the folks stories that are usually spread about the effect of menopause, that menopausal women get crazy, commit suicide because of mood changes that take place in their lives. But all of these leading stories changed, after I saw my doctor and, he recommended the B vitamin family to help built my red cells up, because I suffered from anemia with the next to last pregnancy. I also discussed with some of my neighbors who were much older than I, and had been through the process and was advised by them to take herbs treatment of Valerian and Lydia Pinkham tablets and sage tea.

When I talked to Chila about the strange feelings, I was experiencing, she too recommended the same treatment. I know from personal experience that the Great Physician understands what it takes in each of our lives to restore and sustain us with His healing touch of good health, and He was going to restore my health. It took me some time before it sank into my head that Menopause was bringing freedom into my life. I no longer would have to call the doctor at nights to see our newborn child or because of our children was ill with diarrhea or fever. It was time to focus more on ourselves, because some of our parental responsibility was slowly being relinquished.

Most of our children were already grown, and they could help with the three younger ones. Our two youngest daughters were in elementary school. One of the older boy was starting to have children of his own. I am referring to Armando or Mando who was always in the fast lane, he had a daughter by Gloria Ramon, a few days after I. gave birth to my last child. He named his daughter Julie, who resembled my third daughter Elvia. Armando did every thing in his life time fast. He was the first to get a job, even when he was going to school, he was the first out of three older sons to smoke cigarette and be caught by Albert, and he was the first to get married.

Armando was a very out-going person. Out of all my children, he was the one that I had to keep my eyes open at all time. He would always hang out in front of the yard with his friends, and when he though that Albert was coming home, he would sneak into his bedroom without even washing up or taking a bath. One night Mando was not too lucky, the three boys were already in bed when Albert decided to go to the boys bedroom, and as he entered the room there was a strong foot odor. Albert knew right away who was the culprit Mando or Eduardo, but most likely it was Mando. Albert put his hand under the bed and pulled out a shoe to throw a strike at Mando. Before the shoe could impact against his body he was out of the room and looking for water and soap to wash his feet.

Another one of Mando's tricks took place when he was only six years old. It was on a Sunday morning, and as usual, the children were dressed and ready to go to Sunday School. The Saturday night before, Albert had gave each child their pocket money. I think it was five cents, and he advised they them not to spend all of it. Albert's advised was heeded by them. While I was finishing combing the girl's hair, the boys were ready. Suddenly, Mando slipped out the back door of the house, and went over to a neighbor house where the lady sold goodies. He spent his offering money, and came back without anyone knowing. Once they were in Sunday School, and the offering was being picked up, Mando did not dropped any in. Later on, I found out with the other children, that Mando never put money in the offering plate. He got a paddling and from that day I had no problem with him. These are some of the memories I cherished from my child's early days.

Armando passed away in January 2, 1983, it was very difficult for me to come to New York for his burial. All I wanted was to keep in my mind the memory of him when I last saw him that year early. Mando's death came around the same time that his father died, and I was afraid to have to go through the pain of seeing my son laid out in a coffin. I just felt depressed to talk about this son of mine who in a way I still mourn. All of my children had given me some scar in my life. It is part of being a parent. The generation of today will never have the experiences like myself and my contemporaries. They begin parenthood at a very early age, when they themselves need to be parented.

CHAPTER 11

As the structure of our family was changing, I thought that all was well, when suddenly my peace of mind was disrupted by unforeseen tragedy. It was in the mid-summer of 1955, Chila had an accident while transferring from a boat to the shore on the beach in West End Town, where she attending the burial of one of the prominent businessman Aries Wood. Her foot slipped of the side of the canoe, and she fell and broke her left hip. At that time Chila was 70 years old. It meant that Chila had a higher risk of a full recovery without complication.

Chila was hospitalized for close to a year on the mainland. The doctors put a metal pin in her hip and knee. My two-year-old son and I spent most of the year with Chila. My sister Lolo was still living in La Ceiba. We took turn going to the hospital, and each time we took homemade meals to Chila. She had complained about the unsavory meals prepared in the hospital. America also chipped in caring for Chila, despite her heavy schedule at work in the hospital. Her visits were limited, but she did her best.

During Chila's hospitalization, my younger children stayed at home with Albert and Ms. Florence Bodden, who had lived with our family for many years. When I was away on the mainland, I missed my family very much, especially at night, but at the same time, I had an obligation to care for Chila. Each time I visited Chila, I read the Bible and other religious papers to her, and we shared our understanding of them. One part of the Bible that fully caught my attention was the book of Exodus, Chapter 20, which deals with the Sabbath Day as a sign to God's people. Three families in my neighborhood were know as "Sabbath keepers." These families included the Wilmoth family, Fishers and the Websters. The elder of the Coxen Hole's Seventh-day Adventist Church (SDA) was Albert's cousin, Lionel Wesley, better known as "Daddy Wesley."

The Wilmoth's family lived in a house close to my family. Hilda Wilmoth, along with mutual friends of ours, met in her home to have a midday prayer band. They invited me to join them in prayer for our loved ones. One of the members of this prayer band was my second daughter's Godmother, named Betty Flowers. I decided to give it a try.

At first, I would often forget about the prayer band until, I heard the public clock on the hill strike twelve, and I would hasten out of the door towards Hilda's house. Sometimes, I was kneading my dough to make bread, and I did not have a chance to wash the flower off my hands, or to take off my apron. I just ran out of the house, towards Hilda's house to join the others. It took me some time before I would budget my time in such a way that I was able to be on time for the prayer band.

These moments that we spent together were helpful because spiritually we were blessed. As the years went by, we continued to have our midday prayer band. We came to understand that prayer is communion with God, the fountain of wisdom, the source of strength, and peace and happiness. I also learned more about the Sabbath. It was as if Exodus 20 was unfolding before my eyes.

I am grateful for this provision that God made for me, through my prayer band partners. I found it much easier to have communion with my God, which I felt had a great influenced in me being able to readily accept the message when I heard it under a tent upon returning home from La Ceiba.

After Chila's discharged from the hospital in La Ceiba, we returned to the island. It was now July 1958, the time that crusade or rival meeting is held on the island. The SDA Church had a summer tent set up across the street from my house, and they were holding a series of religious meeting at nights and Sabbath School on Saturdays. This meeting was directed by Pastor Ford, who came from USA to have these meeting. Every night I made sure that I was able to listen to the word of God preached from under the tent. The messages were an inspiration to me. I allowed the Holy Spirit to help me capture the truth about the three Angel's Message to the world. My curiosity was so much, I decided to attend the meetings. I went along with two other ladies, who had grownup in the church but had been backsliding from the church after getting married. At first, Albert was not aware of my attending these religious meeting, because he worked late at nights in his barber shop.

One night during the meeting, Pastor Ford made an appeal for those who would like to take their stand for Christ. Two of my friends and I went to the alter, and agreed to take Bible studies with the pastor. We enjoyed the studies, and they led to our decision for baptism. All three of us were married and had children. It was natural that our husbands had to be told about our decision. We suspected that the news would not be pleasant to our husbands ears. They claimed to be devoted Methodists believers.

After some weeks of Bible studies leading up to the end of the crusade, Pastor Ford agreed that we should speak with our husbands as soon as possible, because that was what God expected of us to be sincere and honest with our husbands. Furthermore, our husbands had a right to know. For one part, I did not had the slight idea, that Albert would have opposed to my baptism, but I was wrong. He was not a person that attended church services regularly, He attended sporadically, which was limited to at least three time per year: New Year Eve, now and then, Good Friday night services and maybe on some special religious celebration. I asked God for the courage to stand up for Him, and to let Albert know about my decision to be baptized in the SDA Church. As I suspected, he got upset. I had made up my mind to follow Christ all the way, and I was determine to pay the consequence. Deep in my heart, I knew that I had made the most valuable decision in life. When Albert and I got married I had thought, that we had made the greatest decision we would make in my our lives, but I was totally wrong until the Holy Spirit of God touched my soul, everything changed.

As the day approached, for my baptism, I made another attempt to share the reasons for my decision to become an Adventist with Albert, but he did not respond. My mind was already made up. So I went ahead. This was one time in my life that I was determined to have my way no matter what the consequence might be. I realized that my soul's salvation was going to be costly. I shared with Pastor Ford what was going on between Albert and me. I felt that Albert's silent was sign of his disagreement about my decision. Pastor Ford questioned me about what was important for me in life and after death. He asked whether it was my soul salvation or my marriage. My two friends had similar experiences. They were not treated kindly by their husbands either. Together we discussed Biblical passages about salvation, and eternity. We found comfort and consolation in them. The pastor also encouraged us to make this a matter of individual daily prayer, and fast and not to forget that Christ had suffered more than what we were going through. His death on Calvary for the sins of the world. It seemed like the more we prayed the relations between our husbands and us were becoming more strenuous.

Some time between the end of August, and middle of September 1958, my two friends shocked me when they told me that they were not going through with baptism. They said they would postpone baptism for another time. I felt sad, and turned to the Bible for consolation. I turned to 2 Timothy 4:7. Like Timothy I was going to finish the race, and keep the faith. I knew that God was there to give me strength. I claimed God's promise, that He would not leave me nor forsake me. God brought me through my trials with Albert. God stood with his arms opened and helped me. Without my daily consecration to God, I would not have had peace nor rest in my soul. God's offers salvation and deliverance to his children and he makes a way for them. God helped me to overcome the internal pain and stress that Albert's actions caused me. Today, I still pray and give God thanks for His tender mercies towards me through my life.

On September 29, 1958, I was baptized. It was a beautiful Sabbath afternoon, when I was submerged in the sea in front of the Little White Seventh-day Adventist Church. What I experienced that moment is indescribable. Only those who have gone to the watery grave of baptism can understand how I felt. The Holy Spirit had taken full control of my life and has helped me to stay faithful and strong in my new found faith. I was striving to develop a perfect relationship with Jesus Christ, my Savior. This made a difference in my life. I was able to understand Albert. I believed that Albert too was feeling the power of the Holy Spirit, but because of his pride and what friends thought about him made him blind.

After being baptized, I went home and there Albert was waiting for me. He stared at me as if he wanted to get a message across to me to indicate that it was not over. Albert shouted, "Damn Seventh-day Adventist." I did not allow his countenance, nor his words to provoke any anger within me. But Albert got more angry when he realized that I was gracefully accepting his verbal abuse. The anger on Albert's face suggested that his anger towards me was not going to be short lived. I prayed continuously for strength, while I did the domestic chores. Often, the devil uses our loved ones as a stumbling blocks in our Christian path-way and Albert had become my obstacle.

I was accused of not being obedient to my husband. Several times Albert told me that what I had done was embarrassing to him. He said that his friends no longer saw him as a "macho man," a man who had no control in his home. I understood all Albert said about his friend's perception but, I kept my belief. Albert was blind spiritually, and could not see that what he was doing would tear our family apart.

These were times when I had questions myself, but I later asked God to forgive me for doubting Him. I was tempted to believe that the price I was paying for salvation was too costly, and wondered if it was worth it. I then remembered the cost that Jesus paid for me before I came into existence. I felt I had sinned. God was there for me all the way; I only had to remain faithful by trusting in Him for strength, and to keep all His commandments, especially the one pertaining to the Sabbath Day.

The Sabbath was Albert's busiest day of the week. He worked from 8:00 a.m. to late evening. Prior to my baptism, Saturday was my preparation day and Sunday was my holy day. I used to cleaned, cooked, and iron the clothes for my family on Saturdays. After my baptism, I spent Saturdays praising and thanking God in His sanctuary. As a commandment believer in the Holy Sabbath, I enjoy true happiness, spiritually and emotionally and I continue to appreciate being in the presence of my Lord and Savior.

I have a commitment to make Heaven my home. I have determined not to allow anyone to deprive me of the Sabbath's blessing. I am very serious about my salvation, and I am willing to pay the price, even it involve losing the most precious and dearest thing to me on this earth. I am willing to give up my Children in order to secure the peace and understanding that God gives to his children. I have struggled very hard for my children, I have given them a nurturing, loving and caring environment to the best of my ability and with God's help. I am aware that at time, I dealt harshly with my children, but all I wanted was to bring the best out of them, but it was difficult for them to understand that.

For many years, I was the only Sabbath keeper in my household. I was very hurt when Albert forbade me to take my younger children to Sabbath School, but I disguised my feeling and this made him angry. Albert's verbal abuse and manipulative behavior became a daily feature. It was worse at night when I shared Bible stories with my children. I continued to pray earnestly before going to bed. I even prayed while I was in bed. I knew what was awaiting me. There were times, when I felt very disillusioned about my marriage and family. I also felt discouraged to the point where I began to suffer from depression.

Often Albert would criticize me in front of my children, and I was afraid, that they would lose respect for me, seeing me as the cause of all the misunderstanding that was taking place in the home. In a way I was to blame, but it was something that made a different in my life. I was able to forgive Albert since I had found Jesus. I learned that when we show act of forgiveness towards another person we are complying with what God requires of His children. In this case the person was Albert.

My God enabled me to recreate in my memory a different image of Albert. I sliced away from my mind the wrong, humiliation, embarrassment, indifference from the person who did it. He was trying to alienate me, but I realized that I had the responsibility for this person to get to know my Lord. I had made a commitment to the Lord to be a light bearer in a world of darkness, in my family, and in the neighborhood. Albert was that dark spot, I had the surety that God one day would take my past, painful life experience, and turn it into a life of joy. This happened when Albert confessed to me that when he saw that I was happy in my religion, and at that time it made him angry because I could share my joy and he did not have anything to share with others.

Despite Albert's verbal abuse, I had a lot to give God thanks for. He did not allow Albert's spiritual blindness to lead him to physically abuse me, like my friend's husband did to them. There were time I felt trapped in my marriage, but looking back, I felt proud that I stood firm in my Lord despite my trials and tribulations.

Day by day, I continued to learn, that every good cause in one's life has a price. I also discovered that we can trust God in the happy and unhappy moments of our lives. God promised not to leave us nor forsake us. He will help us when we are baffled by trials and temptations. "Any persecution that occurs owing our religious beliefs is inspired by the devil, not by Christ" The SDA Bible Commentary (p. 810) states "in the name of religion, many homes have been destroyed, people lose their soul salvation or lose their lives!" To God be the glory for all the ways He has allowed me to triumph in overcoming all the ups and downs in my life. I can glory in my knowledge of God's love for us, which compels Him to search for us. If we accept His offer of salvation. His grace enables Him to forgive us and transform our characters into His likeness, when the latter rain descends. Currently, I am a different person. I am able to exchange my pride for humility, hatred for love, selfishness for generosity and temper for sweetness. All of the undesirable feelings that had arose within me were softened and subdued.

I saw Albert, as I had seen myself, he was a sinner in need of God. I now also had new thoughts and new feelings toward the one to whom I had given my love to. I was a new person in Christ, I cared for the sick and fed those less fortunate than myself.

As each day passed by after coming to Christ, all my past trials were worthwhile, because they made me much stronger to deal with the complexity of daily life. I am still serving my Lord, and looking for-ward to seeing Him in the clouds of Glory very soon along with my loved ones.

My children would often say that they could not sleep at night for my praising God, which was true because He became the center of my life. With Christ in my world it made a whole lot of difference, so I had no alternative but to gave Him thanks. However, as my children gradually began to show interest in the spiritual world, they realized the joy and peace I experienced. They too have learned to express their gratitude to God. I became what some people call the praying lady. I feel very proud to be labeled.

CHAPTER 12

Everything in life has a price. I would like to share one of my most painful moments that took place between Albert and myself. It was on a Monday evening; the midnight moon shone directly on Albert and I while we sat in a hammock on our front porch. The night was hot. It was the summer of 1959. We were enjoying the cool breeze that came from the hills, when suddenly Albert got out of the hammock, and sat on the rail of the porch. He asked me why I continued to make him the focus of laughter among his friends. He said he was getting to the point where he could take no more. I was shocked, and calmly asked Albert, why in the world he wanted me to give up my faith in Christ. I asked him where I would spend eternity if I denied Christ. Albert responded with expletives. He even threatened to divorce me. This hurt my feelings.

My whole life since I was 21 years old had been centered around Albert. I had never imagine that Albert could be so abusive. "God moves in mysterious ways, His wonders to perform." This is my favorite Bible text, and God made a change in Albert's life. He started to be more reasonable towards my beliefs. Years later, Albert confessed to me that he had recognized the change in my life after I accepted Christ, and he too had secretly accepted Christ as his personal Savior.

I often remember the Monday nights in Coxen Hole, when the vessel "Kern," which was owned by the Hyde family, would sail from Coxen Hole to port La Ceiba on the mainland. The vessel transported passengers and a variety of produce. For most part of the night up to about midnight, there was a lot of people trafficking back and forth in the town. People accompanied family and friends back and forth were transporting to the wharf traveling to La Ceiba. On this particular Monday night, while Albert and I were having our heated discussion about my new found faith, some of my daughter's male school mates sat across from our house on a mango tree stump. They heard our discussion, and Albert's threat to divorce me, as well as all the vulgar names I was called. He spoke very loud, and the tone of his voice expressed anger. Albert had become a monster, and I became a victim of his wrath.

The following day, the youngsters in school joked about what had taken place the night before between Albert and me. They teased my daughter that Albert was about to give her mom an ice. They repeated all the ugly and vulgar names that I had been called. When my daughter did not tell me, but I found out by a professor in the school, was how the youngster mocked me. I was so embarrassed. Albert had made our children's lives a nightmare. He had made degrading remarks about me, and he tried to stop me from trusting God, whom he also desperately needed. I have learned that the believer's life is not always joyful, but there is suffering, pain and disappointment. For that reason, I strongly depended on God's word to see me through.

Often many Christians believe that the Christian life is nothing, but a cake walk to heaven. That what my friends and I had believed, when we had first decided to follow Jesus Christ. But as we soon understood the advent message better, I learned that Christians are hated for Christ's name. I learned that as Christian, we should patiently, victoriously, endure the trials of present advancement of God's will on this earth. So my determination was to grow spiritually stronger daily, and to help spread the Three Angels Message. I was not going to turn back now. I had lived 50 years of my life believing that I knew God, but what was missing was a full commitment to serve Him with all of my heart. When the time came for me to fully surrender my life, I did so with no regrets. If I could turned back the clock, things in my life would have been different. I would have sought God at an early age, but nothing in our lives happened before its time.

Years later, I realized that God allows us to pass through fiery trials because He sees something very precious in us that needs refining. He allows suffering and tribulation to smooth the roughs edges of our character, transforming it to be more Christlike. He sure did just that with me. I became more patient, forgiving and tolerant towards Albert's behavior. I know this was only possible, because I relied solely on God to teach, correct, educate and to sanctify me before my husband. I also realized that when we are brought into trial, we should not fret or complain, but subject our souls before God. His ways are of mercy, and the end is salvation. "No temptation has overtaken you except such as it is common to man; but God is faithful, who will not allow you to be tempted beyond what you are able to bear, but with the temptation will also make the way of escape, that you may be able to bear it," (1 Corinthians 10:13, NKJV).

As I grew spiritually, Albert became more and more involved drinking alcohol, which was harming him. He had previously suffered from problems with his stomach, but he was treated and got well. But with his further addiction to alcohol, his health deteriorated further. At night, I often saw Albert take the pain killer "Mejoral" to help alleviate the pain in his stomach. Still, he was too proud to discuss how he felt with me. Maybe he feared that I would use the opportunity to tell him about my God. Albert took pain killers for awhile, until in April 1960 he became very ill. It was a Thursday night when He was rushed by boat to the mainland to be treated. Our oldest son and I went with Albert to La Ceiba. He was admitted in Atlantida Hospital, and remained there for twelve days.

During that time, he showed little sign of improvement. However, on the thirteenth day the doctor advised me to take Albert home, and be prepared for the worse. He was given medication and discharged. The doctor told him to quit drinking, and that he must change his lifestyle or the ulcers would get worse. While Albert was in the hospital, I spent day and night by his bedside praying to God for Albert's life. On the same day that Albert was medically discharged from the hospital, we took the "Julia Vessel" back home in Roatan. The family cared for Albert for at least two months before he felt better, and was able to return to his work, albeit at a slow pace. Even when Albert's work day was short, he still got very tired at the end of the day.

During Albert's illness and hospitalization, he seemed to have done much thinking as he was very close to death. His attitude towards religion changed. He no longer nagged me about the Sabbath, but strangely, he reminded me on Friday afternoon, that the Sabbath would begin in a few hours. I started to see Albert looking at religious literature, which I had purposely left around the house. He would tell me when I saw him reading that he was just wondering if the reading was interesting. I usually encouraged him to give it a try. He usually told me that he preferred to read the Bible alone. Secretly, I thank God for the transformation in Albert's life. It was the Holy Spirit that was working on him, along with the Jehovah Witness' believers that visited Albert in his barber shop, and discussed many Biblical principles, though the principles are somewhat different from what SDA's believe. Albert himself had a lot to thank God for. He spared his life, and his family, and especially our children who contributed financial support. Chila also made a little contribution to help the family while Albert was ill.

Often Chila would send word by someone to tell me to send one of the children up to Goat Hill for something. I always knew what she meant; she either had food or money which she won from playing the nightly "Bolido lottery." Gambling was one of Chila's hobbies, along with smoking cigars. My two sisters also gambled, but I never got involved in gambling because I had to think about my family. Albert had also become involved in gambling, and he gambled up to the night before he died.

Albert was a poor, but proud man. This made him hesitant in accepting favors from anyone, including Chila. I had to put pride aside, and talked strongly to him about his pride. I told him that the family had to help one another, especially when we were in need. God has many ways of providing for his children. In addition, we were concerned about what was going to happen to our youngest daughter, who had completed elementary school. There was not enough money for her to attend secondary school, and we were already struggling with two another daughters attending secondary school in San Francisco and La Ceiba. Albert always told me that I had too big of ambitions, and my ambitions were much bigger than our pockets. I would tell him that we can always depend on God to open doors when we humans feel that our backs are against the wall. Something, miraculous happened. The government planned to open a secondary school on the island, as part of the celebration of 100 years of Spanish rule, but we still did not have enough money for the registration and tuition needed for our daughter to attend.

Unexpectedly, God provided a way. My third son came home two weeks prior to the opening of the education center. It was a surprise and a blessing. He provided the money for the initial fees (25 lempiras or approximately $12.50 USD) as well as two additional months. Our daughter was ready to begin school on April 22, 1961, one day after the centennial celebration. The institute was named "Jose Santos Guardiola" after one of our late presidents.

On April 20, 1961, the community put the final touches on all the preparations to celebrate this grand day. The main street, park, public school buildings, commercial buildings and homes were decorated with flags, flowers and palms. This awakened the spirit of the community for the event. On the early morning of April 21, we were awakened by the sounds of bells on the top of the hill, boat sirens, and gunshot salutations. Motor boats arrived in Coxen Hole harbor from different townships carrying men, women and children. People also came by horse, while others walked to the school, all wishing to be a part of this historic event.

Although we were about to celebrate 100 years of Spanish rule, the celebration had a flavor of the English influence. The celebration lasted all day. It began with a parade, followed by a concert in the park,. There were plays and games which culminated in a dance in the municipal building. Somethings in life seems never to change. The games included the greasy pole and platted pole, which we inherited from the English culture. It was good for us to share with the rest of the community in the celebration, and we were happy that our daughter was one of the first students to enter that school. I was grateful to God for allowing our family, especially eight of our children to be together, and share in this historical event. Little did we know that for Albert, this would be his first and last celebration, because eight months later he was called to rest.

CHAPTER 13

Albert's last eight years on this earth were full of suffering and great pain. He was hospitalized again, because he did not follow the doctor's advice to stop drinking. He completely ignored the doctor's warning, and continued with his habit of alcohol intake with his friends until his stomach could no longer take the punishment, and eventually his habit cause the family a long lifetime lost.

He made a second trip to Puerto Barrios, Guatemala in search of medical attention, and spent four weeks there. When he came back home, he was feeling much better. Still Albert was stubborn, and he did not followed doctor's instruction to change his drinking habits. As a result, three months later in the month of October 1961, he once again started to complain about his stomach. This went on for awhile, and with the help of pain killers, Albert was able to work. Nevertheless, it was becoming visible that Albert's health was declining. His body seemed to be immune to medication.

God was merciful to Albert. He was able to see the birth of his first grandson, whom he gave the name of Rycroff. This was our second daughter's son. We did not approved of the relationship between our daughter and the father of our grandson. We realized though that parents sometimes have to give their children space to make their own errors in life, and to learn from them. Therefore we accepted our daughter's choice with a heavy heart. However, we loved our grandson very much, and the presence of a child in the home helped to take our minds off Albert's health problem.

Our grandson was named after his grandfather, Albert Charrise Connor. I believed in my heart that Albert during his prolong illness was taking a general review of his life. He religiously visited the town doctor's office, and change his eating and drinking habits, but it was too late. He also did things that he would never do if he did not feel his time was short. A few weeks before Albert's death, Albert visited relatives and friend's homes, and even encouraged them to look to a higher being for help in their lives.

Ironically, Albert at first was against me dedicating my life to Christ, but he changed his perception about the SDA church and it's doctrine. He openly confessed to me a few hours before he died that he had accepted Christ as his personal Savior and friend because I had refused to give up my belief in my new found faith, and my commitment to serve God. Even when he tried to force me to abandon it, he said he could not understand what motivated me to tolerate his verbal abuse. Albert, added that he did not feel the need to make a public confession, but it was between him and his God. His confession to me made me feel proud of how I allowed my God to used me as a partner in shedding light before him. All I could do was praise God for hearing and answering the long hours of prayers by my church family

December 30, 1961, was a gloomy Sabbath day. As usual, Albert got up, dressed, and ate his breakfast. He was on his way out of the door to confront a very busy day. The day before the New Year Eve, men were looking forward to having their hair groomed for the big night. My second son was very humorous with the neighbors,. He joked about the years end by saying that the old man would shortly die, and all must get ready to bury him. This was an innocent joke, but it took meaning for our family on the following day.

Before Albert left the house on the morning of the 30th, he kissed me and I saw in his face pain and fear, but he was determined to go to work despite my suggesting he stay home and rest. Albert's response to me was that a man has to provide for his family, and the woman he loves. He added, "Nana, you know that."

Albert tried to smile, but the discomfort was there. He said, "Nana tomorrow is Sunday, I will stay home, and at night we will go to the Church for watch night service." I agreed with him. Albert made his way out of the yard, and I saw how difficult it was for him to walk and just maintain a straight body posture. Right away I knew how much a strain it was for him just to put one foot ahead of the other. He was using the last of his physical strength just to make his way toward his shop. As I stood there looking at Albert, chills ran down my spine, and fear invaded my body. I could feel that all was not going to be alright. My greatest fear of death had just seemed to be becoming a reality. Immediately I sent a secret prayer up to the God of the universe on behalf of Albert's well being.

After Albert left the home, I cleaned up the dishes, and got ready for Sabbath School. Again I whispered a prayer, committing my family especially, and Albert to the Divine will and care. I prayed, "O Lord, thine will be done and give me the strength to deal with whatever you have in store for us. Grant the peace my heart is seeking. If Albert is to continue to be a provider for his family, please give him the strength. Amen." I knew deep down in my heart that God answered my prayer at that moment. I began to feel a wave of blessing that thrilled me through and through, and brought tears of joy and gratitude to my eyes. I had a strong sense that my petition had reached God's throne, but the meaning of the response I did not know.

Many questions plagued my mind. Would Albert's health improve, and his life be prolonged? Would he be able to see his three younger children Susana, Guillermina and Terrell grow up? Would we be able to enjoy our golden years together? The nearness of the Divine presence raised my hope that it might be so, since Albert in the past had been able to overcome his health problems. The rest of the Sabbath morning past uneventfully. I enjoyed the midday sermon, "God's Promise to His Children." It seemed like Daddy Wesley knew that I need to hear such a message. It strengthen me spiritually and I was able to understand better that no matter what life brings to us, God is still on our side. After the service, I told a few brethren that I would see them in the afternoon. I went straight home, and as I was entering the yard I met with a young-ster, who gave me a note from Albert. The content of the note was to inform me that he was busy, and to please send his dinner by the bearer of the note. He added that he intended to keep his promise for the next day. I smiled to myself, and hurried to prepare a tray with food to send to Albert. The rest of the family and I had dinner without him.

The rest of the afternoon, I spent time with the church brethren, visiting the elderly and sick in their homes in the neighborhood. We also shared some religious literature with people on the street. The evening was cool and it looked bleak, so we decided to returned to the home of one of the sisters in Christ to culminate the Sabbath Day with whisper, and then return to our respective homes.

Albert was punctual in coming home. He did not appear to be hav-ing pain like he had had earlier that morning. I prepared supper, and we sat around the table and asked God's blessing upon our food. I went into the kitchen to bring Albert's favorite cake, which he called "War Cake," because it reminded him of the years of the depression when we had to use brown sugar to sweeten ever thing.

After dinner the children did the dishes. Albert and I went to the porch to relax from his hard day work. Albert promised the children that after they finish cleaning up the kitchen, he would give them money to go to the movies. This was strange, because he did not allow them to go to the movies, especially at night. We sat on the porch until the children returned around 9:30 that evening, and then they went inside to get ready for bed. For a while, Albert and I lay in bed, and we talked about what were going to do the next day. He suddenly turned toward me, and kissed on the cheek; his lips felt very cold. I asked him if all was right. He answered affirmatively.

I fell asleep a short time later, but was awaken by Albert's body trembling. It was almost midnight. I go up and asked Albert if he needed his medication, which I gave him, but it seemed like he was not getting any relief. I called for my second son Eduardo (Wavi) and daughter Ruperta (Perta) to come to our bedroom. Before they came, Albert told me that he wanted to go to the porch, and that perhaps the cool air would help relieve his pain. He claimed that his stomach felt like it was on fire. I called for my son to go and let Dr. Polo know what was going with Albert. He came back with some pain killer tablets. Albert took the tablets, but nothing happened. He continued to get worse, and started becoming delirious. Albert stated to me that his mother and father was sitting next to him, but both his parents had been dead for at least 60 years or more.

When our younger children came out on the porch and saw their father talking out of his head, it made them scared. Albert looked at them, and called for them to came to him, but I could see the fear on their faces. My first thought was to assure them that all was right with their father, and they must go back to bed and sleep. I sat next to Albert trying to help him control his body, and at the same time I was silently sending heavenward my petition for guidance.

Suddenly, I realized that the special morning blessing that was given to me was to steady me for this hour of need. For the next few hours I clung to a thread of hope. Albert seems to be taking control again of himself. He said to me, "Nana, you must be tired. Go and lay down for awhile in the bed." and "I will go and sit in the rocking chair in the living room next to the radio, if I should need you I will call."

Before we left the porch, our neighbor Mr. Clark Wilmoth was passing by on his way home, and saw us and came to inquire what was going on. I explained, that Albert was having one of his stomach attacks. Mr. Clark took hold of Albert's wrist as like he was taking his pulse, then he turn to me and said that Albert was dying. He could not find his pulse, and he told Albert that he should have a last drink before he died. In the interim, my next door neighbor Raymond McBride came to see what was all the talking about at such an early Sunday morning (about 3:45 a.m.). Raymond said that maybe it was best for us to go inside the house where it was warmer. We followed his advice, which Albert had earlier suggested.

We entered the house, and I went to our bedroom, and Albert stayed in the living room. I closed my eyes for a short time, and may have possibly fallen asleep, but suddenly I was awaken by the sound of someone chocking. It was now about 5:30 a.m. I jumped out of bed, and ran toward the living room where Albert had been sitting down, only to see him struggling to breathe. I screamed and called for Perta and Wavi to come. My scream was so loud, that my neighbors McBride, Price, and Webster came immediately to see what had happened. The neighbors tried to give Albert CPR, but it was useless. Albert had already expired. This happened on December 31,1961, Albert promised me that we would spend the whole day together, and then go to the church services at night.

As the news of Albert's death spread, Dr. Polo came to the house. He reminded us that he had said Albert was not going to live much longer after his last stomach attack. His inside was eaten out by the ulcers. A short time later, Chila came down the street to be with us. She took control of the house, which gave me some time to think things through. I was glad that Chila was there for me.

Now Albert's body immobile. His words from the day before kept popping up in my head, "I will rest all day and then attend watch night services." I was grief stricken, but I realized that I had to be strong for my children. All the past memories about my brother, dad, grandma, and my daughter, now were revived in me. I had a sense of loss that human sympathy can lighten, but never to remove. I took control and came to grips with myself, and realized, that there was no more we could do for Albert. The sense of the finality of death was beginning to set in as the hours went by. The fear of death was now a reality. Never again would I hear Albert's voice, "time to get dinner Minunga," which was his nickname for me. Nor would I have to remind the children that daddy will soon come home. I would never again hear his cat like soft step coming in the dining room or bed room, calling my name and asking if the children were all right, or listen for his breathing when I woke up at night.

Albert might have felt that death for him that day was eminent. Only if I had got the message, I would have attempted to pursue him to stay home, for us to spend his last day on earth together. Thirty-two years of joy, struggle, and hardship of raising a family of nine had suddenly came to an end. Albert was not the perfect man, but he had a great quality that he made sure that his family was provided with what the Good Lord promised his children, "bread and water." Now it was my turn to assume the job of the provider of the family. I would have preferred to become the provider under other circumstances, but God knows what is best for us.

We now had to make plans for Albert's burial. Around nine o'clock, one of Albert's friends, Eugene Brown, came to the house with a yellow envelope, which he gave to me. He said that Albert left it with him the night before, and asked him to deliver it to me the next day. I was curious about the contents of the envelope, and I took it and opened it. The envelope contained Albert's barber shop keys, some dollar bills, and a few pieces of the lottery ticket. Later on I found out from some of Albert's friends that Mr Brown had told them that he kept for himself some of the lottery tickets, that Albert had given to him for his family . It is true that when people are vulnerable other people take advantage of them. At first, I felt anger towards this person, but I asked God to forgive him, for what he did, and to forgive for me being angry. I also realized that Mr Brown was not obligated to gave me anything, but he did. The funds in the envelope were enough to make the necessary arrangement for the funeral the same day.

In Roatan it is customary for people to bury their dead the same day, because funeral parlors were not popular. My personal opinion is that it is best that we take care of burial the same day because it helps the healing process to take place, than having the corpse for days, and the family having to think about when will be the final moment they will see their loved one.

It was winter, on a Sunday evening at about 4:30 p.m., when Albert's body was buried in the cemetery at the "Barrio El Ticket." Despite of the weather conditions and the night celebration to bring in the New Year 1962, people from various townships came to pay their last respect to the man whom they considered to be the best barber they had ever known. I remembered many times when Albert and I had come to give our respects to friends who had passed away. We were like most families; when it comes to death, we did not want to face it, but we all too often surrounded by it daily through the news media, and by what is going on in our environment.

Our family, like most families, have experienced some tragedy where one or more have died. On that evening, I had many thoughts running through my head. I thought how Albert's record was closed, not for ever, but until the day of resurrection. When we go through the "valley of shadow of death" (Psalm 23:4), the value of life seems to increase in our minds. To us Christians, the message and good news of the resurrection becomes even more real when it involves a loved one .Oh, how we need to be ready for that glad day when death will be turned to endless joy, when Jesus "will transform our lowly bodies; to be conformed to His glorious body" (Philippians 3:21). With that consolation in my mind, I reflected on my own life, and thought how my own records were still open. While Albert is sleeping, I reassured myself that I would by the grace of God live a Christian life, not only before my children, but my friends, so they too can have the privilege to enjoy the good news of salvation, and be able to experience that transformation of the body - whether alive or dead on that great day.

In my hours of bereavement, I found support in my church family and in the Holy Words of God, which gave me hope to believe in the future after death. The messages on death and the return of Jesus in the Bible was like food to strengthen my spiritual soul. They have been the source of my support during the difficult days that awaited me. I must now adjust to my role as widow, single parent, and bread winner for the family. Through His word, the Good Lord instilled in my mind that in the midst of bereavement and tears, it may seems short term but the physical absence is long term and it is for keeps. I did have my moments of fear and doubt, but I soon realized like the apostle Paul said, "I can do all things through Christ who strengthen Me" (Philippians 4:13).

My faith in Jesus Christ provided a double portion of the health, strength, and determination to comply with my role of single parent. As human beings, we have to accepts that in everyone's life there will be some experiences that are inescapable tests. The bereavements, sickness, pain and loss which I have experienced are tests that seem impenetrable to our understanding and reason, yet, God's purpose always comes through, bursting from behind the darkness of our grief.

CHAPTER 14

A few days after Albert's death, I soon realized that things were not going to be easy. I continued to depend on the Lord, who silently revealed to me one of His many plans that He had in stored for me. This plan came to me while I was laying down in bed on a Sunday afternoon in 1962. God put into my mind the idea of going into the cooking business like Chila had done. It would be a mean steady income to support myself and my children. As for customers, I thought about the school teachers, who came to island to teach in the public schools. These individuals had a monthly steady income, and would be the best demographic to focus on. Part of the puzzle was being solved, but the next part was much more difficult to solve. It involved money I did not have. I needed to purchase extra tables and chairs to accommodate at least six to eight customers, and to provide them food.

On the next day, I shared my idea with one of the businessman. He offered to gave me a line of credit, and I accepted his offer. A few weeks later, I opened my cooking business. I had such high hopes, and such great plans for the future, when I first opened my business. For three and half years, things were going well for my family. I was meeting all the family's financial obligations, and was even able to save a few lempiras. Unfortunately, things began to change. Competition started popping up, and the number of customers started to reduce. Other families in the neighborhood were going into the same business as I had. They wanted to share what they believed to be a money making business.

At first I was upset with the families in the area that were taking away my business, but I soon realized that I was over reacting to the whole situation. We all were struggling to make ends meet in our homes. I found myself in a predicament. I was spending more than I was making in an attempt to retain my customers. I was not able to meet my monthly expenses. I was falling behind in paying my daughter's tuition, and getting her ready for graduation in November. Finally, I realized that, I had to act fast, if I wanted to see my daughter graduate. So I decided that I would bake breads and cakes to sell every day. This turned out to be a successful effort. I would get large orders for bread daily from two of the stores in town. I also got orders from some of the people in town. With what I made, and what I received from my children, I was able to catch up on some bills.

In the first years of the 1960s, life was not too kind to many family. Husbands were dying, and leaving big family and without any financial provision. However, God in His own way through my church family and close friends came to my rescue. Often we were blessed by their generosity. They were practicing the "religion," that Brother Paul speaks about in the Good Word, "Pure religion and undefiled before God and the Father is this, to visit the fatherless and widows in their affliction" (In James 1:27). The Preacher said, "Cast thy bread upon the waters: for thou shalt find it after many days" (Ecclesiastes 11:1). In other words we need to put the needs of others first, and our own need last. This behavior of giving to others in need had been practiced in our home, as I stated earlier. Many years before I had come to know the Lord as my Savior and friend, I had helped my neighbors and even strangers with the little we had.

Unconsciously, the Spirit of God was working within me. He was helping me to understand the big controversial issues from Biblical times of, "Who is our neighbor?" from the story of the "Good Samaritan." When Albert was alive, he was hesitant about extending his hand to strangers, however on one occasion Albert went along with me to provide some practical help for a couple, who lived out of the town of Corozal, and were visiting Coxen Hole when the husband got sick. We opened our doors to them. We shared our home, our bread, and our water with them, until the husband regain his strength, and was able to return to their town. This was not just an act of mere sympathy, but as an act of kindness, and an expression of one of the fruit of the spirit.

My third son did not view our behavior favorable, because he had to give up his bed for some time. He complained that our family did not have enough to share. I explained to him about the universal law of giving. We do not lose by giving, rather we increased our capacity to give as the Lord blessed us. After Albert's death, the help that our family received was the return to favors previously given to others. It was our family's time to receive God's blessing.

God always blesses in abundance and in miraculous ways. One of the ways that He blessed my family was with a bread fruit tree that grew in our backyard. This tropical tree only gave fruits once a year, but after my baptism, I pledge to make it a part of my investment plan to the Lord. It bore fruits all year long, which was very rare. The fruits grew much larger than usual, which meant I could sell each one for more, and my investment funds would also be more at the end of the year. The fruits also served to provide some food on our table, as well as enough to share with others. For years, this tree produced fruits, and it survived numerous hurricanes. I learned a very valuable lesson from this bread fruit tree after I had first became a true Christian. We have to trust in God, believe in His Word, and accept the way that He works in our lives. At times we can never fathom is love for us. We should ask the Holy Spirit to give us the wisdom, knowledge and understanding of how God works, which is in a mystery, His wonders to foretell. I learned from this tree that in God's hands, every things just multiply.

Another way that God had blessed our family was by allowing me, along with my daughters, to be able to make crochet table cloths, doilies, and bedspreads to sell,with the help of other family members. God not only blessed our family with material things and emotional support, but with the opportunity to see three of my daughters prepare for baptism. They were all baptized into the Seventh-day Adventist church six months after Albert passed away.

June 9, 1962 was a Sabbath Day, and I was bubbling with joy and thankfulness to my God for having the privilege to set the right example for my children, and for them to follow in my foot steps three and a half years after my own baptism. It was a thrilling moment for me to see my girls emerge into the watery grave. It brought back memories of the feeling of calmness and peace that I had experienced. I was so happy and thankful to God that my daughters did not have to be subjected to the opposition and trials that I had to go through with Albert. What a remarkable difference it was for them to publicly take their stand for Christ. They had all the moral support that I did not have. This made a whole lot of difference in their decision.

Oh, it is so wonderful to be able to be free to serve the God of the universe. Nevertheless, my family received some criticism by some of our neighbors. This is a typical characteristic of small town dwellers. After all that I had been through with Albert, I did not let any remarks about my children's decision get me upset. Remarks such as, "if Albert Connor was aware of what was going on in his family, he would roll over in his grave." Little did these neighbors of mine know that Albert had confessed to me that he too had received Jesus into his life. He no longer would have opposed our daughter's decision. I would have preferred for Albert to be alive and to share in this event in his children's lives. Thirty-two years of married life is not easy to forget. However I have hope, along with my children, to see Albert on the great resurrection day when Jesus return.

As I look back on my life, I realized that if Albert did not die, I would not have been able to experience one of God's promises to widows and orphans to provide for all their needs. Our family lived day by day, praising God, for the tender mercies that He bestowed upon us. We shared our church activities, without any fear of being reprimand. My children and I no longer had to pretend that we were going to different church services, as we did while Albert was alive. For instance, on Sunday nights, I would take my hymnal and Bible, and leave for Sunday's night service held at the Adventist church, but my children were prohibited by Albert to go along with me. They were told, that they had to attend the church services held at the Methodist Church. Albert made sure that his order was obeyed by the girls, so what he did on Sunday nights was to sit in the living room next to the radio, as the girls marched toward the door with the Methodist Church Hymnal in hands. This was only a pretension, because they were on their way to the evening services at the Adventist church. Once they were out of the house and into the street, they would then go to the back of the yard and climbed over the fence and into the back door of their bedroom and retrieve the Adventist Church Hymnal, leaving the Methodist Church Hymnal, and we would meet in the church. After the service was over, they returned the hymnal to the back bedroom and picked up the one that they left there, and enter the front door. This went only for some time. If Albert had only knew what the girls were doing, God knows what he might have done to them. God always makes a way for His children to meet and study His Word.

My daughters and I became active in our church activities. I became elected as Sabbath School Superintendent for may years. My children also held various offices in the church. I feel that one of the most rewarding activities in our church was the yearly Harvest Ingathering during the month of November. This gave me opportunity to be a witness for my Lord with some of the same families that had criticized me when I get got baptized. This was a blessing in itself, because some of these people became interested in the message of salvation, and I was also spiritually was enriched. I continued to participate in the Harvest Ingathering each year that I was in Coxen Hole, Roatan.

CHAPTER 15

During the next few years, my family continued to grow, especially between the years of 1962 and 1965. God blessed me to be able to see three of my daughters get married, and to see five of my grandchildren born: Albertina, Avenell, Suyapa, Rue, Dacia and Wade, and to see three of them dedicated their lives to God in my faith. I thank God that three out of four of my children that were baptized remained faithful. The rest of my children are from a different religious persuasion, including the Roman Catholic, Episcopalian, and the Church of God faiths. They serve the Lord, but I pray to my God that they too will one day accept the, "Three Angels Message" that is exposed in the Book of Revelation. I am aware that no denomination is going to save our soul, but only our faith in the true and only God, creator of mankind.

My overall spiritual side was strong, but my financial side was very limited. I was confident God was going to make away, I did not know how I was going to comply with my daily responsibility. Economically, I was still having some difficulty, but spiritually, I was stronger than ever. Behind every dark cloud, so the saying goes, is a silver lining. God was just waiting for me to ask for His help with all my needs. It was the end of March 1966, on a Sunday afternoon, I was sitting in my bedroom, and I was having a hearty conversation with The One who knows me best, and loves me most. I told my best friend what was going on in my family life. I had two children to put through school, and things seemed to be very dull. I wiped my tears, and shortly I fell asleep. About an hour before the sun set, I woke up and from my bedroom window, I saw a gentleman, Mr S., an old family friend, coming into my yard. I was surprised and taken back when this young man called out my name, to see him. I greeted him and he delivered me a letter from my daughter in New York.

We conversed for sometime about our family life. I felt the need to talk with another human being about what was going on. Normally, I would not have poured out my heart to anyone. Mr S. smiled, and said that he thought that the contents of the letter in my hand would be the answer to my situation. He was sure that it contained good news. How correct Mr. S. was! I did exactly as he suggested, and was thrilled. My daughter suggested, that she was going to send papers for my youngest daughter to migrate to the USA.. At first, I thought it was a good idea, but a second thought ran through my mind. If I was able to come to the USA, I would be able to work and send money for my children to continue with their education. I also would be able to rebuild our home, which was needed badly. I was aware that God was the source of all temporal as well as spiritual blessings only if I kept my mind absorbed on heavenly things and not on worldly things. Often we fail to exalt Christ, and we are yielding to Satan's devices. I was not going to let my ship of life sink. A ship does not sink when it is launched in the water, it sinks when water gets into the ship. I was not letting this opportunity pass me, I needed to launch my ship into the waters.

My problems was great, and if I did not take charge of them, my ship would have sank, but there was someone who was in authority. I had God, and by His help, I was willing to take the risk. I said to myself, look out world, here I come in God! It was not easy to launch out to a new start, but I had to do it along with God, because He had a plan for my life and I know it was good. With God as a partner, the difficulties were overcome. Often I would cry secretly, and I would talk to my Maker, and trust that it was the right move. How could I ever distrust God, and fear that He will leave me to want? Where would my faith be? Our heavenly Father feeds the ravens, and will He not much more feed me and my children.

After my conversation with God, I felt a peace and calmness that invaded my whole being. I knew immediately that another one of my prayers was heard. Right away, I got busy. I looked for paper and pen, I sat down and wrote a letter to my daughter, expressing my plans, and hoped to mail it the next day. Later, that evening, when my married daughter Elvia, visited me on her way to evening church services, I shared with her the good news that I received, and the plan I had in mind. She agreed with it, and promised to care for my two youngest children if everything worked out as planned.

The next day, I also informed Chila about my plans. Chila was happy for me, but at the same time, she had a mixed feelings about me leaving her. I was her only relative that remained on the island. She was advanced in age. Maybe she was afraid of the idea of being alone. At first, I was a little taken back. I too had reservation about leaving my Chila and my children, but it was something I had to go through with. One part of me was telling me to stay, and the other part was saying go. So I followed my later feeling with the help of God. I let Him lead my life and with confident that this was an opportunity to provide for my children's future. I could not disregard the plan. I remembered how Grandma McKay and Uncle Henry were not afraid to leave their country in search of a better life. I got the courage to work on my plan. At least, I had an idea about the country to where I was planning to travel, but Grandma and Uncle Henry did not have a clue about Honduras when they had moved.

In the middle of April, I received a letter from my daughter agreeing with my plan. She informed me that she had submitted an application for my residency to the Immigration and Naturalization Services in New York for processing, and that they would get in touch with the Embassy in San Pedro Sula, Honduras, about the status of the application at the indicated time. I continually prayed to God, that all thing to go well with my papers.

On June 3 1966, I got a notification from the American Embassy in San Pedro Sula, Honduras, advising me about the status of my application, and I also was informed about the documentation I needed to bring to the embassy by June 15, for an interview. On that date, I was granted visa for residency in the USA. I returned home and told my family and friends the news. I had a month to prepare myself, and make sure that everything for my children was in place, before my departure to New York.

A month later, early in the morning of July 12, 1966, I committed my family to God, and with a heavy heart, I got dressed, and finished packing suitcase. It was time for me to leave for the airport, and to say good bye. At 5:30 a.m., when I was leaving my home, there stood a few of my neighbors in my front yard, waiting to accompany me to the airport to start out on my journey to New York.

Along with family and friends, we walked to the airport, where I would board the National airline of Honduras, "Shasta" in Roatan, at 6:30, with a destination of San Pedro Sula International Airport, "Villeda Morales." At the last call for passengers to board the plane, we hugged, kissed and clung to each other. It was very emotional moment for me to say goodbye to my loved ones. I had to be strong. I entered the plane, and I took my seat next to a window. I silently thanked my God, and asked Him for His blessing during the flight. I repeated my favorite Bible verse from the book of Psalms 121, known as the traveler's psalms. Before the airplane took off the runway, I had a last look at my children and friends. They were waving their hands to me. Suddenly, I felt overwhelmed by my feelings. Inside, I was yearning to be with my family. I felt tear drops running down my cheeks. I was not sure if they were tears of joy or sadness.

In the past I had traveled to the mainland as well as the other islands, but this trip was different. I was going thousand of miles away from my family, and I realized that it was going to be a very long trip, to a country I did not knew, except what I was told by my children, friends, and pictures that I had saw of the United States..

I arrived in San Pedro Sula approximately at 8:00 a.m. We stayed on the airport until 1:00 p.m., before the national airline announced the flight to New York's International Airport, "John F. Kennedy," arriving at 6:00 p.m., where I was met by my daughter Olimpia, and her husband, Hover McKenzie, as well as my two oldest sons, Tomas and Armando.

I lived with my daughter, my son- in-law, and my grandson Wade Albert on Bushwick Avenue. During all the planning for my trip, Albert was always unconsciously on my mind, and even more on the day of my departure. Most likely, if Albert was alive, he would not have agreed for me to travel, and leave my family behind. He seldom traveled except for medical reasons.

After being alone, my thoughts went back to my flight. Once the plane was in the air, I had sat starring into the clouds. I reminiscenced about how my grandma McKay and Uncle had felt when they departed from Belize back in the 1800s. I never believed in my most remote dreams, that one day I too would be going far from home. I knew for sure, that my God had His hands in every movement that I made. He was directing my feet towards a path that would allow me to provide for my family's needs. I also had many pressing thoughts that kept running through my mind. I was still continuing to adjust to the "single parent" life, my daughter's graduation from "John F. Kennedy Secondary Institute," and my baby son was finishing elementary school at the "Juan Brooks" Public School. While I sat there thinking, I must have fell asleep only to be waken up by the flight attendant announcing our arrival to Kennedy. It was a pleasant flight. It was just the beginning of many trips I would take in the future from New York to Honduras, and vice versa. When I came to New York, I had already completed my 58 birthday. I was not a young women, but I had goals for the future. God blessed me shortly after I arrived in New York with jobs, a new church family at Mount Of Olive Seventh-day Adventist Church, located on Hopkins Avenue, and many new friends.

My first job was assisting an elderly woman in Coney Island. It was five days a week, far from my home, and it lasted for only a short time. Deep inside of me, I knew that my God had something better in store for me; something that was closer to home. My feelings were accurate. I left my job in Coney Island the end of August on a Friday afternoon. The following Monday, my daughter's friend advised me that I should look for work at the "Home for Old Age" across the street from our apartment on Bushwick Avenue.

On Monday, my daughter took me to the home so I could fill out a job application. In those days jobs were not hard to come by. We found out that they were in need of workers to start to work immediately. I was scared to be exposing myself to an environment that I was not familiar with, and if I got the job, it would be the first time working in an institution. Only a few minutes after completing the job application and handing it to the secretary, I heard my name called to come to a specific room. My daughter and I went together, and I was interviewed by the manager Mr. Carlmicheal, and his supervisor. Mrs. Ann Bigger who later became my close friend, maybe because of our age and our strong religious beliefs. They inquired if I would be able came to work on the following day, which was Tuesday. I did not hesitate to give my answer affirmatively. Right away, I was advised to visit the health center on Wilson Avenue to have a physical done. I was given a package containing a white uniform, and a pair of shoes. I was told to be back at 7:00 a.m. sharp Tuesday morning. Everything was happening so fast around me; all I could do was to secretly praise my Lord, for His blessing upon me. This job lasted for six full productive years.

It was September 1966, at 5:30 a.m. on a Tuesday morning, the day after labor day, and the weather was comfortable for the beginning of Fall. It was going to be my first day on the job at the nursing home, I got out of bed, took a shower, dressed in my white uniform and sat down to read my Bible, and to talk with my God.

I had breakfast with my daughter. I felt a little bit scared, but I had to go and confront the real world of work. I said to myself, "world here I come" as I was leaving the apartment. I walked across Bushwick Avenue, and entered the home for the aged, where I was greeted by the head nurse, Ms. Ann Bigger, who introduced me to the staff, and informed me about the ward I would be assigned to. I was then taken to the floor and introduced to patients and nurses on the East Ward.

My work schedule was from 7:00 a.m. to 3:00 p.m., Monday through Friday and some Saturdays. At first, I felt like I was breaking the Sabbath Day, but I remembered that Jesus did good on the Sabbath Day. I made a promise with my Heavenly Father, that my earning for the Sabbath, I would give it to the church as a special offering.

Caring for others was not new to me, and my greatest concern was if I was going to be able to perform a good job. I was aware of my ability to care for others, and it came natural, but now the situation was different. My co-workers, especially one of them by the name of Josephine, were very helpful. They spend time showing me some of the things I was not familiar with, such as the different equipments, their functions, and how to use them. I was very appreciative of their help. It was not long before I was helping the new workers, who started after me. I knew my God was with me, and He was going to see me through. My plans was closer to providing the financial support to send back home, and I was seeing my dreams become a reality, which was to see my daughter finish at "the John F. Kennedy" secondary school, and to send my last son to the Adventist boarding secondary school in Pena Blanca, San Pedro Sula. I also wanted to start rebuilding my family a new home.

I wrote to my second daughter, and asked her to go ahead, and look for a carpenter and get an estimate of what it would cost to rebuild the house. Two weeks after I started to work, I received my first paycheck. All I could do was to praise God for His continued blessings upon me and my family. I went with my coworker to the Roosevelt Saving Bank on Gates Avenue to cash my check. The night before, I had made out my budget, which included, my tithes, a few dollars for Chila, my daughter in school to get ready for graduation in November of 1966, and my second daughter to put in the bank towards the construction of the house. Once a month, I would send money home, until there was enough for the carpenter to start building the house.

This went on for a year and a half, until I had accumulated enough money to be able to start the construction of my house. All the arrangement were made by my children for the foundation of our new home to start. Another one of my dreams were becoming a reality, and God was the one that made it happened. Little did I know that I was making the arrangement for my third daughter to pass her last days on this earth in some comfort. This subject has been set aside, and in the future it will be given it consideration.

CHAPTER 16

Three months after I had moved to New York, the cold hands of death struck again. My daughter Ruperta had given birth to my granddaughter a few months before my departure from Roatan and in September I got the news of her death. It opened old wounds about my own loss of my little Margarita. I gave the Lord thanks for giving me the pleasure to be able to hold in my bosom that little bundle of joy. One month later, on October 20, 1966, I got the good news that Elvia and Brent had had a pair of twins, a boy and a girl who they had named after themselves.

The twins were an addition to the previous two children they had already had. I also received a copy of my daughter's Mina graduation invitation, and gave God thanks for His blessing to me. I proudly told my co-workers about the great event that would take place on November 28, 1966, when my daughter would graduate with a Teacher's Certificate. I felt proud to see another one of my children living out my dream for them. As the months went by, the holiday season was approaching, I was going through another emotional turmoil.

It had been five years since I had buried Albert. It was the first year that I was not going to spend Christmas with my younger children and Chila. It was my first experience dealing with snow, and the very cold weather. To make matters worse, we had a very bad snow storm in New York that year. I shed many silent tears, and inwardly, I was yearning for my loved ones. I longed for the warmth of the sunny days back in Roatan. Yet I was grateful that my children in New York did their very best to make me feel at home. Still, a mother's love for her children is very strong. I thought about how God must have felt when He was separated from His son, Jesus, by death for my sins and the sins of the whole world. Only love can make the difference, and I loved my family. I was determined to continue to make sacrifices for them by the help of God. For two years, I did not see any of my family in Honduras.

We maintained communication by letters and telephone calls, which I enjoyed very much. In July of 1967, I got news that Mina was suffering from severe headaches. Although this was not strange, I was concerned about what was going to happen to her. I sent money for her to go a see a Doctor in Tegucigalpa after a recommendation of a family friend She spent a few months under treatment, and then returned home. In all of this, I knew that God hands was directing my path.

In the summer of 1967, my daughter informed me that we had accumulated enough money to rebuild our home, and the carpenter was ready to start. I could not thank God enough. Back in New York, my daughter and I started to shop for things for our new home. I visited many stores, especially when there was a special sales, like on the holidays. Time flew by so quickly, that before I knew I had another granddaughter, born on November 7, 1967. The child was named Juana Georgina, after me and her father's mother. Soon the Christmas of 1967 was here and gone, and it was time to plan for vacation time in the spring of 1968.

In June 1968, I had taken an earlier vacation than I had planned because I had received news that Elvia was very ill. She was better known as Blackey because the color of her skin was much darker than the rest of her siblings. She had long black curls prior to her illness.

On Sunday morning, June 12 1968, I left from John F. Kennedy Airport for Honduras. I arrived on the Island of Roatan that afternoon. I was shock, when I saw my daughter in such poor physically condition, despite of all the medical attention she had been given in Honduras and Belize. My children were renting a house next to ours, while our home was being built. It was almost finished, but I could not wait to move my daughter into our unfinished home, so that I could take care of her. I received help from my church family and old friends to help us move. They also helped me take care of Elvia. She had lost a lot of weight, and was bed ridden. Doctors had already given up on her. They were unable to diagnose what was the cause of her illness. When I saw Elvia, all I saw was death. I spent a lot of time with her, and even when she was unable to talk, I knew she was aware that I was there. I prayed for her daily, and hoped that God would have mercy on Elvia and spare her life. I wanted her to be able to care for her children, and see them grow up, but that was not part of God's plan for her.

On June 28, 1968, at 6:30 p.m., Elvia closed her eyes and gently slipped away to be with her Maker. It was a Friday evening, and the Sabbath was beginning. At that moment, I felt like my heart had broken into many pieces. Sometimes my thoughts ascended to God in a melody of praise, for relieving my daughter from all of the pain and suffering she had been going through. It was one of the most hardest moments of my life when I looked at my four grand children who had lost their mother.

They were between the ages of one and half years old to five years old. Elvia was buried on Sabbath evening at 4:30 p.m., next to her father in the cemetery in the Ticket. During Elvia sickness, Brent had been away on the sea.

Unfortunately for Brent, he did not get to see his wife alive. He arrived the next Sunday from Miami after Elvia had been buried along with Terrell, who come from Pena Blanca. A few days later, Brent decided that the two older children Sofia (5 years old) and Avenell (3 years old) would go live with his relatives in the United States. Avenell went to live with Brent's aunt Enid in Boston, and Sofia went to live with his sister Sara in New York. The twins were also separated.

Brenda was going to live with Ms. Felicita Fortado in Sandy Bay, and Brent Jr was going to the Price family in Coxen Hole. I would have liked to care for my grandchildren, but I had a lot of unfinished business to accomplish. My house was not completed or furnished, and Terrell was still in school. As a parent, I did not want to inferred with Brent's decision of who would care for his children. Before the children were separated, they spent some time with me and the rest of the family, before I returned to New York. I enjoyed ever moment of it. The separation was painful, but I had to accept it and continue on. Terrell returned to Pena Blanca to continue his education. He was in his second year of "Plan Basic" at the Seventh-day Adventist college.

Chila and I had the opportunity to spend some good time together. We talked about the past when we all lived on Goat Hill and below in Grandma McKay's house. We were amazed how things had changed on the island. Since I had left for two years previous, we now had an active airport, and cars covered the streets. There was many more people moving in from the mainland, and the demand for housing was becoming very great. A few days before I returned to New York, I was approached by a lady inquiring if I was going to rent any rooms in my house. I had no plans to rent my house, because my children were going to stay in it.

Chila and I also talked about Don Juan. Chila expressed her concerned about him. He had left Roatan seven months previously, and headed for La Ceiba on the mainland. She had not heard from him, and everybody she had inquired with could not tell anything about him. I offered to take a trip to La Ceiba, and to see what I could find out. My trip was not successful. I found out from old friends that there was a possibility that Don Juan had proceeded to the Mosquita Coast, in search of relatives there. At the time he had been seen, he appeared to be acting very strange. It was not very encouraging news to take back to Chila.

I was not sure how Chila was going to accept this news about Don Juan. He had been around Chila since he was teenager. He had become an integral part of our family. I considered him as my older brother. Chila was up in years, and she was living alone. It was hard for her to not know anything about Don Juan's whereabouts. In addition, she had recently lost her great granddaughter, and I was about to return to New York in a few days. My heart ached for my daughter and leaving my aged mother was most difficult. I would have given anything to be able to stay with her. Leaving loved ones behind is like an emotional roller coaster. One is so torn; happy because you are there with them, and on the other hand, sad because it is time to go return to continue making a living. I consoled myself that I was completing my house, and securing something for my golden years. My sense of independence has always been the force that keeps me going. I knew that my children would share with me some of their income, but I did not want them to feel that they were forced to care for me.

On October 24, 1968, I left Roatan for New York's John F. Kennedy Airport, where I was met by my children. My son Armando said that he had a surprise for me. He showed he my own apartment located in his building. I moved my belongings from Olimpia's apartment into my own.

I spent a few days before I went back to my job at the nursing home. At first it was difficult for me to be around the elderly. Each older woman I cared for, I saw Chila, and when they talked about their daughters, I remembered my daughter Elvia. Many days on the job, I would go to the bathroom and just let myself cry out for a while. Elvia's death was still fresh in my mind. The emptiness in my life was very painful. The absence from my daughter, and separation from Chila seemed almost unbearable. One day as I spent some time in the bathroom, I was discovered by my supervisor, Ms. Bigger, and she prayed with me.

I began to relive memories from my past every time one of my patients got ill. A fear often invaded me that the next thing that would happen to them would be the cold hand of death, and their families would go through what our family had. I was aware that God was with me, but in my weakness I felt helpless as if I neglected my daughter Elvia. Oh how I wished that I would have been in Roatan to have spend more time with her during her illness, but life's circumstances had not allowed me to do so. I thank my God that He is the one that knows the future of His children.

CHAPTER 17

As a parent who has lost an adult child to death, guilt was eating me up, but time had to do the healing. My pain was gradually decreasing, and I started getting used to the idea of some of my family being gone, I started to focus all my energy on my work. I tried to work double shifts, so that I could earn more money. I wanted to bring my son Terrell to New York, and move into my own apartment. Terrell was about to finish school in Pena Blanca, and I wanted him to come and attend school in New York. I knew that my Savior was going to intervene, because all my prayers were becoming realities. I rented an apartment in my son Armando's building on Bushwick Avenue, which I furnished with the basic furniture until I was able to do better. My daughter Sue was staying with me for a while before she returned home.

During her stay in New York, Sue's son Rue stayed with a couple of his aunts in Roatan. Together we shopped for different housing items and cloths for her to take back home for my house in Coxen Hole, as well as a few things for the rest of family. Sue was also expecting her second child, which she would have back in Honduras. She left New York for Honduras in the mid-fall, and shortly thereafter gave birth to a girl child, whom she named Cynthia Geniva Bodden.

Christmas was just around the corner, and I received some information about a boat called, "Judith," which was owned by the Hyde family. This ship sailed between Miami, Florida and Honduras, and one of my youngest daughter's schoolmates worked on the vessel. I made contact with the office in Miami to find out the date that the boat would be coming to Miami, and returning to Honduras. They informed me that the boat would docking in Miami on December 15th. I bought additional clothing for my children still living back home in Honduras, and shipped them to Miami, addressed to the Hyde's boat that would be returning to Roatan. I also sent communion utensils for my church in Coxen Hole, along with my tithe money.

I celebrated the holiday season that year with my children and grandchild in New York. This brought back memories of Albert's death. The New Year started out with a lot of snow, but this year I was able to cope a little better than the two previous years. It seemed like the snow was not going to stop falling. I thought about springtime, which kept me hopeful that I would soon enjoy a beautiful fair day. Yet, I knew deep down in my heart that spring, in all its beauty, was not coming any time soon.

The winter months were moving along, and soon March arrived with it's breeze and sporadic snow. I returned home from work one Sunday evening in the month of March, and my daughter informed me that Perta had called to let us know that Chila was sick. It was five months since Chila and I had seen each other. When I left her, she was active and did not show any sign of slowing down physically or mentally. She was still taking care of herself, and her business-cooking which has been her life-long career. Surprisingly, one never knows when to expect sickness to knock at their door. While my daughter sat in the living room, planning for my return trip to Honduras, my first thoughts went back to Elvia, for whom I was still mourning. Silently, I sent up prayers to Heaven on behalf of Chila's health, as well as my safety. I was especially concerned that I would not be able to see Chila alive again. My thoughts were interrupted by the telephone ringing; it was my daughter calling from Honduras. She gave me full details of Chila's illness. The family Doctor, Policarpio Galindo, had diagnosed Chila with a stroke on the same side where she had broken her hip broken some years before. It had affected her right side as well as her speech, but she was still a alert and aware of her surroundings I told my daughter that if I was able to get an airline ticket for that night, I would be in Coxen Hole the very next day. It had already been a week since Chila had her stroke. As I hung up the phone, I became very concerned about Chila. I had seen too many elderly people suffer stroke during the time I had worked at the home. Many of these elderly folk never recuperated. Chila was elderly, and the chances of recovery was very slim, so I was quite eager to return home.

My daughter told me that she was going to call Tan/Shasa Airlines, and purchase a round trip ticket to Honduras. Fortunately, I was able to get a reservation on the plane leaving at midnight from Florida, where I would make a connection for Honduras early on Monday morning. I made a telephone call to my supervisor, Ms. Ann Bigger, and informed her about the emergency trip to Honduras to see my mother. I requested for the time off, but I could not give her a definite time because I did not know what to expect. She was very understanding about the nature of my request, because she too had an elderly mother residing in the nursing home. She did not hesitate to give her approval, and told me she would take care of all the paperwork.

I called my two sisters living in New Orleans, and told them about Chila's illness. They immediately made plans to travel that night to Florida, and to take the first airplane the next morning to Roatan. If the circumstances had been any different, I would have been elated to see them in Coxen Hole, whereas my mind was consumed with concern for my mother. After I hung up the telephone, I packed my suitcase with a few necessary items and clothes.

As I waited for my flight, I thanked God for His blessings, and my ability to get a seat on that airplane. I gathered the few dollars that I had kept in the apartment for emergencies, along with what my daughter and sons had provided. It was just enough to pay for my airline ticket. In those days, a round-trip ticket to Honduras cost only $399.00, but over the years I have seen the cost of a ticket to Honduras rise to at least $575.00. I also had a saving account in one of the banks on the island. Everything seemed to be falling into place.

My daughter, her husband, and my two sons went to the JFK Airport with me. My ordeal was about to begin. The plane was scheduled for departure at 12:30 a.m., with a destination to Miami International Airport. Three hours later, we arrived in Miami and departed for Honduras at 8:00 a.m., arriving on San Pedro Sula's International Airport, "Villeda Morales." I was now only an hour and half away from home. While I was waiting for my departure to Roatan, I was surprised when an announcement was made by the tower, advising passengers that a storm was heading towards the island of Roatan. It was said that it would affect the north side of the island. Since we would not be traveling along the south coast of the island, it would not affect us. Unfortunately, it did not happen as it was announced by the airport's weather bureau. I trusted my Lord that He would take care of me and the storm, since He knew what my mission was.

Once the plane was in midair and half way to the island of Roatan, the whole plane started to shake. The pilot made an announcement that we would not be descending in Roatan because of the weather, but rather we would be heading for the airport in Guanaja. He added that we would have to spend the night in Guanaja, and see how the weather was in the morning. We were directed to go to a hotel in the town until the next day. I tried to contact my my daughters in Coxen Hole, but wasn't able to reach them.

Back then, the telephone system in Roatan wasn't the best, so I went to the wharf and asked the captain of a fishing boat to send a message over the radio for my children. It was the fastest means of forwarding information at that time. He granted my request, and I went back to the hotel and went to bed. I was so exhausted from traveling the night before, that I slept through the night. The next morning, I got up early and was ready to start my journey, but was informed that the storm was not yet over. Then I remembered hearing the night before that some men on the fishing boat had mentioned that they would be sailing to Roatan the next day. Another gentleman who was going to Roatan and I went to the wharf, and inquired if the boat was still going to Roatan, and if it was possible for us to go with them. We were informed by the captain that they would be sailing at 10:00 a.m. sharp, and if we wanted to take a chance, we would be welcome go along.

They informed us that they were only going to the town of Oak Ridge, and not Coxen Hole. He suggested that we could possibly find a motor boat going to Coxen Hole, or some other means of transportation to take us there. We decided to take the chance, and left Guanaja at 11:30 a.m., arriving at Oak Ridge three hours later. It was a frightening experience. The sea was infuriated, and the boat rocked back and forth. While I sat on the edge of my bunk, I thought of scenes of Jesus and His disciples when they were on the sea of Galilee, and Jesus was asleep during the storm. His disciple were scared for their lives, and at that moment I shared their fears. I cried out to God to please bring us safely to our destination. When we arrived in Oak Ridge we found that nothing was going to Coxen Hole by sea or land. There was nothing else to do, but spend the night there, and early the next day, which was Tuesday, the sky was blue. There were no signs of rain and the sea was calmed. As one author says, "After the storm comes the calm."

We left that morning from Oak Ridge in a motor boat heading towards Coxen Hole. I was so glad to arrive. I immediately headed to Chila's house. She was alert and recognized me, but was unable to talk from the stroke she had previously suffered. I embraced her and she too, responded. She took my hand in hers and she squeezed it very tight, and gave me one of her big smiles She also made some effort to sit up in the bed, but she fell back. I spent the day with her before going to see my own home. Later that evening, I returned to spend the night with Chila.

The next afternoon, Lolo and America arrived on the plane from New Orleans. By now Chila was not as alert as she had been when I had arrived. She seemed to be getting worse each day. For four days she remained unconscious, and on Easter Sunday March 28, 1989, in the late afternoon, Chila fell asleep. She was buried on Monday afternoon in the cemetery, "Mount Hole." After Chila's burial, a family feud broke out between my siblings. They were looking to see if Chila had any valuables, money or property documents. Unfortunately, she only had one document for the land where she was living. Chila had trusted a neighbor with her money, and when he was asked, he told us that he had returned everything to her. Only God knows if he was telling the truth, but not long after Chila's death, this neighbor had a nervous breakdown, and died soon after.

Chila's funeral was a big one. People from different towns on the island of Roatan came to show their last respects. Most of them met Chila because of her cooking skills, her generosity, and her common sense in home remedies to preserve good health.

One thing I can proudly say about Chila, is that she had a heart as big as the world. She did not think twice about helping another person. If anyone would came to her with their problems, she would not hesitate to lend them her hand, whether it was by giving them the last spoonful of food in the house to a hungry person, or giving the dress off her back to someone who needed it. She would share with new mothers some of her secret tips about caring for a child who may have had a flu or any health problem. Her behavior resembled the Biblical character, "Dorcas," who when she died, was deeply mourned for her kindness to the less fortunate than herself.

Chila's loving and caring attitude towards others were embedded in the lives of all of her children. I too was gifted with this same behavior. My children had a hard time sometimes accepting how I would always sharing with others the little that we had, but has they matured, they began to understand what the Monarch of the Universe requires His children to do, "to cast your bread upon the water." He blessed me over and over when I least expected it. I would received my blessing from a friend or a family member, or even a mere acquaintance.

Positive comments about Chila did not end after her death, but continued for many years after. During my trips back to Honduras, I would often be approached by some of her old friends who would mention how she had done something good for them in a moment most critical in there lives. To listen to these comments made me feel very proud of her.

I knew I could never measure up to her "kind deeds," but I sure would give it a try in my own humble way.

After Chila was buried, Lolo and America returned to New Orleans a few days later, and I stayed with my children for a month before I returning to New York. I felt an inward peace just to have been able to be there for Chila in the last moments that she spent on this earth.

On April 24 1969, I returned to New York, where I resumed my job at the nursing home. Even though I was emotionally torn apart by Chila's death, I managed by God's help to find some comfort in being around the elderly for whom I had grown to develop a special love. I felt like they were a part of my family, and some of them I also shared the same feelings of a special bond between a mother and a daughter. I was confident that my God was there for me, and He would provide all the strength that I needed to carry on with my goals in life.

The decade of the seventies was much better for me than the previous decade. Four of my children came to the United States. In 1974, I brought my grandson Rue Mann to New York. We shared the apartment until Terrell came no long afterwards and a few months later, Mina came just to visit for a while, returning to Honduras a few months later. She returned to stay in 1978 along with Ruperta, her husband Alfredo Rodriguez, and their youngest daughter Nubia. The rest of her children remained in Honduras until a future date. I was proud to have my two younger children with me for awhile, as well as my grandchildren, which awoke in me feelings of earlier motherhood when Albert and I had worked so hard to raise our children. We not only had to provide food on the table, clothes on their backs, a roof over their heads, but we were willing to go the extra mile in order for each one of them to have the opportunity to fully develop intellectually to their full potential, and to be all they wanted to be.

I was now realizing my dream that all my children would receive a good education. Terrell was the last of my children to finish school. He enrolled at Franklin K. Lane high school, where he graduated, and decided to continue at Stoney Brook College. This child of mine seemed to have problems with deciding or exploring his vocational calling. He kept moving from one state to another, traveling through Arizona and Colorado, before finally moving to San Diego, California, where he enrolled in Berkeley Law School.

In May 1988, he graduated with a degree in International Business Law. My daughters, Sue and Mina, and I attended his graduation in

California. Years before, in October of 1978, I visited San Francisco, and it was the first time in almost six years that I had seen my son Terrell face to face. I had the opportunity to met his girlfriend Jane, and her son. Business Law had not been my plan for Terrell, for when he was born I dedicated him to God in a special way. I wanted for him to be a minister; I wanted him to spread the word of God, but it did not happen. Terrell was the only child that I have shed many tears for. Often I did not know if he was dead or alive, until I would receive a telephone call or a postcard from him somewhere in the country. Still, I never stopped praying that God would continue to bless him, and bring him back into His fold.

Sometimes I would question myself to see where I had failed in raising him. I had treated him no differently than I had treated my older children. The only thing I could think of was that I had left him at an earlier age than any of my other children. In addition, when Albert passed away, I was left alone to be the sole bread winner for the family. After anxious searching of my soul, I came up with the conclusion that I did my best for Terrell, and it was up to him to follow my instruction. I committed him into the hands of the Lord Almighty to take control over his life. I thought about the parable in the Bible about the prodigal son. He did not do what his parents expected of him, but in the end he returned home. I knew that one day Terrell would do the same, because of the foundation we laid in his life. Perhaps I won't be alive to see it, but I had the confidence that he would surrender his life to God one day. As long as the Lord blesses me with my faculties, I will continue to pray for my prodigal son, as well as the rest of my family..

The decade of the 1970s had been more of a blessing for me than disappointment. I was surrounded by most of my children now living in New York, and I had five grandchildren born and three great grandchildren during this time. The good Lord was still blessing me with offsprings as more grandchildren were added to my family in the following years. It was a coincident, when in 1971 my oldest son and my oldest daughter, both had their last child, Tomas Jr. and Guillermo Armando. While I was enjoying my blessings, I took a vacation with my son Armando in June 1971, and we traveled to Honduras for a few weeks.

Unfortunately, during my visit home I had an accident that nearly cost me my life. I was home two days after Armando came back to New York, and I was standing on a chair hanging a curtain in my living room when I fell and injured my left leg on the hand rest of the chair. I went to see the doctor. He saw how bruised my leg was internally, and decided that it needed to be drain, which he did. It seemed that this made matters worse. Two days after the procedure, my whole leg turned black and blue. I returned to see the doctor, and he suggested that I need more intense treatment, and I should immediately return to New York.

I quickly got in communication with my children, and Armando decided to come and bring me back to New York. I was taken to the Jewish Hospital on Prospect Park and soon admitted. I was told that gangrene had set in, and I was very fortunate to be at this hospital, otherwise I might have lost my leg. The doctor at the hospital had to reopen the incision to drain my leg, and inserted a tube. I spent 15 days in the hospital before I was discharged. I moved with the help of crutches until my leg was completely healed. I never doubted that Christ was going to restore my health like He had done so many times in my life. While I was hospitalized, I thought about the time when Chila had also broken her leg. I was out on sick leave for a while before I was able to return to work. The next year, I had another health problem about the time when I was going to celebrate Rue's birthday. Despite all the setbacks that the evil one was trying me with, I did not plan to give in, because my God was not going to let me get discouraged and give up. I knew I was going to enjoy all the blessings that He had bestowed upon me.

CHAPTER 18

My life in New York not only consisted of work and broken health, but also many pleasurable moments. I became familiar with many of the tourist sights in the Big Apple, such as the Empire State Building, Stature of Liberty, Rockerfeller Center, Coney Island, and the famous Bronx Zoo, Central Park, the Cloisters, Prospect Park, Staten Island Ferry, Circle Line, Flushing Meadow Park, Yankee Stadium (to see the Brooklyn Dodges play, of which I am a diehard fan), the Broadway Show, Fiddlers on the Roof, Macy's Easter and Thanksgiving Parades, St. Patrick Cathedral and many other historical places. I also took trips with my church, Mt. of Olives, to other estates such as Danberry Fair Park, Pennsylvania Dutch, Bear Mount, Forest Parks, New Orleans, Chicago, Boston, New Jersey, and Canada, etc. On some of these trips, I took along one of my friends from the job by the name of Constance James, who became my traveling buddy for a while until we both retired and went our separated ways.

January 29,1972 was a Sabbath afternoon as well as my grandson, Rue Mann's birthday. It was about 3:00 p.m., I was leaving my job at the nursing home, and on my way out of the building. The steps were covered in a thin sheet of snow, as earlier that day it was snowing and by noon it had turned into ice. I lost my footing as I was leaving the building, and slid down the steps. As I fell down, my head hit the railing, breaking my glasses. A piece of glass penetrated my left temple. Before I knew I was surrounded by co-workers in attempt to help me get up. By now, I had blood all over the front of my white uniform, and running down my face. I was so scared, that I yelled for help and got a quick response. My supervisor, Ms. Bigger, called the ambulance, and then she came to my apartment and told my daughters about the accident. Someone would have to go with me to the emergency room when the ambulance arrived, so two of my daughters accompanied me to Ridgewood Hospital. In the emergency room the doctors removed the piece of glass from my face, and sewed up the area. It was a long stay at the hospital.

We had planned to have a family celebration at the close of the Sabbath for Rue, but now I was in the hospital. I did not want to disappoint

Rue, so I tried to be positive as we managed to sing Happy Birthday and share ice cream and cake. I did not return to work for many weeks. During this time, I received workman's compensation. While I was healing from the accident, my troubles did not stop there. A few days later, Mina became very sick with the flu. She had major chills and a fever. I believe this was the result of her being exposed to the cold weather the day of my accident. She also caught bronchitis which kept her in bed for the next two months, before she showed any signs of improvement.

For days all I saw in Mina's face was death. I immediately forgot about my own physical pain, and was scared of the thought that was going through my mind. The idea of having to face the death of another child was more than I could handle. As my custom was, I prayed to God for her recovery, and I truly believed that it would come. It did. I do not want to exaggerate, but my prayers were heard in a matter of seconds. Before I even got off my knees, I opened my eyes and saw Mina's eyes open. She asked me for something to eat. I welcomed God's miracle-working power. Just the two of us were in the apartment when it happened, and I shouted for joy with tears running down my cheek, praising and glorifying my Savior.

At the time when we were are going through sickness, the evil one tries to put doubt in our hearts about God, who promises never to leave nor forsake us. God has commanded us in His word to ask, seek, knock, and give thanks. I have learned from past experiences that we need to be confident when we call on God. No matter where or when we call upon Jesus Christ, our intercessor, we will be delivered from the power of evil. Only by earnest and sincere petitions, in accordance to God's will, will our prayers be answered. Every day I thank God in prayer for His Lordship over death, which is our greatest enemy, and for His Promise to intervene when we call to Him, believing in Jesus, "the resurrection and the life (John 11:25)."

During the time I was home on sick leave, rumors were circulating that the nursing home was closing, and some of the residences were going to be sent to different facilities, but the majority of them would go to Long Island. Later I was told by my supervisor that the workers had options of taking a buy out, or applying for jobs on Long Island. Those who were eligible for retirement should take it. Myself along with others up in our sixties saw this as an opportunity to get out of the labor force. I discussed the situation with my son Armando, and he was in favor that it was time to take it easy, since I had worked so hard raising him and his siblings. He contacted the social security office, and got the application for social security benefits.

A few months later, I retired on social security disability and have begun enjoying my golden age by the help of God. During my traveling within the USA, as well as back and forth to Honduras, I have met some of the members from the "Merry Bee" club. All of us had retired from work, and we made plans to have a picnic to spend sometime catching up. It was a thrilling reunion to be able to see childhood friends again after so many years of being apart. It brought back good memories of the time we shared growing up in Coxen Hole. We were like teenagers when met, after all, we had not seen each other for a long time. We spent time remembering how our life was in the past, and how it was then.

Interestingly we no longer looked or thought like we had over 50 years or 60 years ago. Mother nature had taken her toll on our bodies. Mentally and physically, we have changed. Our minds wavered at times, and we now had a lot of wrinkles on our faces. We had gained extra pounds through our bodies. When I got married, my weight was 99 pounds, and now I am 165 pounds; what a big difference. Our hair had turned silver, our eyesight diminished, and our bones creaked when we walked, but we were happy. We realized that we had to give God thanks for spiritual blessings, health longevity, financial and material blessings. Most of us had established a good relationship with God, we have seen three generations. We had moved from not having enough to meet our daily needs, to having more than enough to share with others, owning homes in USA or in Honduras.

One thing among us did not change completely, our eagerness and undivided attention to gossip. As human beings, there is always the temptation to listen to gossip. I personally feel that a little constructive gossip, if there is such a thing, is not wrong. But it is wrong when we add to what we heard, and spread it around. For two weeks we ran into each other. We made sure that we exchanged addresses and telephone numbers, and promised to maintain contact after returning to the USA.

This vacation was one of the most beautiful vacations I had among the numerous ones I had experienced. Nothing is more gratifying than to be able to share all that God had done for you. How He brought you from a life of sin into one of hope. I am very grateful, and will always be to God for every moment in my life, and for all the abundance He had provided for me and my family. By His help, I am enjoying the rest of my life to the fullest. I know that one day all of my joy on this earth will come to an end, and I will have to go to rest like Chila, some of my children, and many loved ones.

The following years, my old friends and I ran into each other in New York, New Orleans or in the airports traveling between Honduras and New York. Since my retirement, I was always on the go. I was told by one of my sons-in-laws, Charles Thompson, who in humor told me that I should consider buying an airplane; this way my trips may be cheaper. I agreed with him, and told him that I was as free as a bird. Responsibility as a mother and a wife were finished many years ago, and now I was on God's time. I did not fear death. In my lifetime I had experienced a lot of people dying. I was confident that God was going to take me to rest when He saw it fit, so I was enjoying my life to the fullest.

CHAPTER 19

My traveling was not only confined to my birth place in Coxen Hole, Honduras, but to others states there, and in the United States. I visited the states that played a historical role as far back as the 1300s. The Mayans Civilization cities of Copan and Ocotepeque, and the two capitals. The old one Comayaguela and new Tegucigapa. The Ruins of these cities have deeply impressed me because of the Mayans people's great abilities and dexterity in the construction of these cities, with their awesome buildings and monuments created with limited tools. God had blessed them with an extraordinary intelligence.

In November of 1976, I had the privilege of going on a tour of the cities with the Baptist church congregation for 15 days. I was amazed to enter these ruined cities, to see and touch artifacts from the past. It made me think about the Holy City that God has gone to prepare for His people. Just to think about the day when we will be taken to that heavenly city, the New Jerusalem, with it's streets of gold, makes my whole being rejoice and yearn for that day to come. I have feelings of ecstasy to see the Heaven City. In July 1982, I visited the Holy Land for 21 days with the Northeastern Conference. This experience was breathtaking; I was in the land where Jesus my Savior lived thousands of years ago, and for me to be there walking on the streets where Jesus walked was such an indescribable feeling that I hope to remember it as long as I live.

Day after day we traveled to different countries such as Athens, Turkey, Egypt, and Israel. As we visited various sites, our tour guide explained their significance. The Bible became alive for me. At night I would lay down in bed at the hotel, and just let my mind wonder about the magnificence of the day. I thought of the Isle of Patmos, where Brother John had his encounter with the Heavenly Beings, who revealed scenes of the last days in Revelation, chapters 20–22. My heart warmed as we visited the Bethlehem manger, where Christ was born, and the Garden of Gethsemane, the opened tomb, and Golgotha. My blood shivered to know that this was where God's great love for this sinful world was demonstrated, when He sent Jesus Christ, His only begotten Son to died for my sins. King Solomon's temple of gold made me think of the city of gold that awaits all of God's children when He returns. At the River Jordan where Jesus Christ was baptized, I took off my shoes and stood in it looking towards heaven as the disciples did watching Jesus being raised up into the cloud.

This trip was surely a link that brought me closer to my God, and the burning desire to see my family join me in serving the one and only true God. I always had a close relationship with the Father, but at the beginning of my walk with God, I strived to have even a closer relationship. I am sure that by His help, I will remain faithful to the end, so I will be a part of the great multitude that Christ will return to take to the Glorious Heavenly City. One very exiting moment during this tour was when a faithful pastor from another denomination, who was traveling with us, openly confessed that the Seventh-day Adventist denomination are people that follow the commandments, and he wanted to by a part of us. This Pastor was none other than David Glover, husband to Hazel, who was already a Seventh-day Adventist believer.

God blessed me to hear this dynamic pastor preach on many occasions. This Pastor is proof of what the Holy Spirit can do in our lives. After I returned from my Holy Land tour, I spent the balance of the summer in New York before I returned to Honduras. During my stay, my children decided that we should file a petition with the Immigration Naturalization Services on behalf of my son, Eduardo, to obtain legal residency in this country. Eduardo was the only one of my children still residing in Honduras. It was natural for him to have the chance to visit the United States. I knew that I was going to miss Eduardo if he was granted legal residency, but still I wanted him to have this opportunity. For many years, he and I had been together. I knew I would miss Eduardo's cooking, which he did especially well. Sometimes Eduardo would wake up early in the morning, and come to my bedroom with a little "trago," or a cup of some beverage. Now I had to give him the same chance as I had given the rest of my children. Many years ago, when I started to have a family, I made a promise that I would never stand in the way of my children when it was for their best interest. Therefore, I resigned to the fact of Eduardo coming to USA. I knew that God was going to provide for me as He did in the past.

In November, 1982, Two weeks after I returned to Coxen Hole, Eduardo got notification from the American Embassy of a interview scheduled for November 15. I was happy for him, yet sad because the time had come for me to be alone. Two weeks later, Eduardo came to New York, just in time for him to spend a few weeks with Armando, who celebrated his 50th birthday on January 2,1983, and was called to rest by his Maker after battling diabetes for many years. It was a Sunday morning when I received the call from New York about Armando's death. At the time I was alone, and I felt like my whole world had come to an end.

My first reaction was to call out to God for help. I felt robbed again, as I was going to bury another one of my children. I could not understand the law of nature anymore. It seemed that the family roles had been reversed. I the parent was burying my children, rather than the children having to mourn for me. Only God knows why it was happening to me. I dared not question God since I have put all of my trust in Him, but I had a right to express my grief. I had ambivalent feelings about coming to New York. One part of me wanted to be there, but I was afraid of seeing my son's cold and immobile body stretched out in some funeral parlor. The other part of me wanted to cherish seeing him walking and jolly with his bearded face. Mando had been a good son. As the saying goes, the good one always die young. So I made the choice not to come to New York. I was glad that Eduardo, Armando and the rest of children were able to be together prior to Mando's death. I think my biggest fear was that Albert too died on a Sunday before the New Year. Every time death strikes, it brings back memories from the past, despite the many years that have gone by.

The year 1983 started out with sorrow and grief, but the fire to work for my Lord was still burning within my heart. Not a day passed by that I would not look for someone passing my house in the corner of the Barrio of El ticket, to tell them about my Lord. I became more involved than I had been before migrating to the United State back in 1966. I felt a strong conviction that God wanted me to support His cause in the Coxen Hole SDA Church. I fervently assumed my role as the Sabbath School Superintendent and the Ingathering and Investment Leader. It may seem that I was selfish, but it was the Holy Spirit that had changed me, and I did not forget that I had to work along with the pastor of the church as well as the other members. Maud, a sister in Christ, and I planned to do missionary work in the area where we lived, located in between two bridges called Big Bridge and Small Bridge. There we launched an aggressive campaign in the community.

Our target audience was the adults and even strangers. Most mornings, Maud would be the first to approach our targets with religious literatures, while they passed her store, and a short time later, as they approached the crossing road, I would be the next to present them with the Word of God. If for any reason I was not able to witness before 8:00 a.m. with these prints, I made sure that I would be standing at my post in the afternoon before 5:30 that evening. Later on in the day, Maud and I would meet in her store to discuss the individuals we had contacted that day. We both agreed to select two professors and a Doctor who had recently came to Coxen Hole to work in the public school and in the health center. God's hand was in our work. The two professors were Arnulfo Agurcia and Mario Lanza, and in the past they had been our daughters Mina and Rolita's teachers while they attended the secondary school in Manuel Bonilla and San Isidro Institute, as they lived on the mainland in La Ceiba, and the Doctor was Miguel Arias who was a classmate of my daughter (Mina) in the Manuel Bonilla Institute during the mid 1960s.

At first, these individuals did not show any interest, maybe because they were brought up attending the Roman Catholic Church. Yet, as the days and weeks went by, we noticed that these individual's attitude changed toward us when we interrupted them on their way to work. Perhaps they tolerated us because of our age and gender difference, but when they saw us, they would ask us, "did you pray for me?" They may have said it as a joke, because every encounter we had with them, we would end with, "I will be praying for you," and they would smile. It seemed like they were becoming amicable toward us.

One day they said to me, "what topic do you have for us today, is it about heaven or hell?" A big smile spread over their faces, and I started to believe that the seed was being planted in their hearts. So it gave me the opportunity to invite them to come to our church for Bible study with our pastor. I was not surprised when they accepted, because the Holy Spirit was working on them. Maud and I, as well as the rest of believers were also praying for a harvest of souls. We were not as successful with the doctor, but we continued to pray for him that he would too yield to God.

In the summer, I made my usual trip to New York, my second home, to visit the family, but before I could returned back to Coxen Hole, the two professors had openly accepted Christ as their personal Savior and friend and were baptized. Both Arnulfo and Mario were married, and had their family living in La Ceiba and San Pedro Sula. When I went back to Honduras, they were still working on the island, and they shared with me some of their experiences with their wives and children. I too shared some of my personal experiences when my husband and I took my stand for the Lord. Maud shared what her family had been through with her father. We continued to talk with the new converts about all the sacrifices a human being can make, yet it does not compare with the sacrifices that God made for this world on Calvary. They were invited to participate in our midday prayer, while we promised to pray individually for them and their families. Our support seemed to help them understand the choices they have made to walk the narrow path of life which leads to life eternal.

A year and half later, Mario gave us the good news that his wife and children have accepted Jesus as their Savior, but Arnulfo was still praying for the salvation of his family. The Doctor was like King Aggripa, he was almost persuaded to believe. I know that the Holy Spirit had planted the seed, the word of God, in his heart, I pray that one day the doctor will surrender his life to God. If we allow the Holy Spirit to lead us, we can lead others to know Him. For years we recruited other members to participate in the street ministry.

In 1985, I came to New York to make preparations to attend the Seventh-day Adventist General Conference, which was to be held in New Orleans, in July. Along with my daughters Ruperta, Susana and Mina and two of Susana's friends Carol and Karen Williams, sisters, traveled to attend 10 days of the meetings. While we were in New Orleans, my son Terrell and his friend Ms. Lynette Parker came to see me.

This was my first time attending a gathering of such magnitude with representation from different countries in the world. The messages presented in these meetings were powerful and inspiring to the faith. It was very touching to listen to how the "Three Angels Messages" is being accepted by great masses of people who at one time didn't believe in the Almighty God. Now so many are coming to God. I met distinguished individual and groups like H.M.S. Richards Sr and Jr., the original founder of the world wide radio religious program, The Voice of Prophecy. This is one of my favorite religious programs that I have pledged to financially support over the years. I met the King's Herald Quartet, and got their autograph on one of their record. One night while we were in the hotel in New Orleans and was already in bed, we had a scary experience. One of the girls was taking a shower, and the steam from the hot water triggered the fire alarm. Before we knew it, the fire truck was outside, and the firemen with their hose was banging on the door yelling for us to get out. I scrambled out of bed, and grabbed my shoes and pocketbook and ran down the stairs. The hotel manager changed our room to another floor, but somehow the fire alarm in that room also went off as well. By the time we finally got to bed, it was three o'clock in the morning.

Another shocking experience happened the next morning as we were about to take the city trolley down to the Superdome Stadium, where the meetings were being held. Sue and Karen boarded the car; I was about to get on it. My hand held the door knob, but before I could put my foot in the door, the car started to pull out. For a moment I was running along side the car with my hand on the door knob. It seemed like my hand was glued to it, and I could not take it off, for fear of falling down. I screamed along with the rest of the girls that remained outside, as well as the two that were in the car. It was an early morning commute on the streets of New Orleans. Finally, the car stopped, and the door opened and the rest of us got on. I arrived at the stadium trembling, but as I sat for a while I tried to regain my composure, and was ready to receive the blessing of the day. Between breaks, we took time to enjoy the Forth of July fireworks along the Mississippi River, French Quarter, and the old Bourbon Street restaurant. We also had time to visit my sisters and some old friends from back home.

I like New Orleans very much because its tropical climate is similar to Honduras, and the numerous Latinos that reside there. However, they most likely are from Central America. This had been one of the states beside New York that I have visited often. It was also the home of my two sisters, Lolo and America, which never came to visit me in New York.

As a believer in Christ, I had to show my sisters about the love of God that was within me. They never took their religious life seriously. They tried to hold on to both the church and to the worldly pleasures that caused my sister Lolo her health in 1988. I made my sister's lifestyle one of my burdens. I yearned for them to experience a closer walk with God. I wanted them to share the habit of daily happiness. So my daily custom is to present them before the throne of grace no matter where I was.

In the fall of 1985, I enrolled in Brooklyn college to take a course on CPR. It was one of my earlier dreams not only to participate, but to live the experience of attending a University like this, I wanted to have the experience like my children had. That year I attended Mina's second graduation in the USA at Madison Square Garden. When the day came for me to go forward to receive my certificate of completion of the course, I was elated. Myself and another elderly woman were close to celebrating eighty years, and were were now experiencing our adolescent dream. I was proud as a bird "quetzal" when he spreads out his feathers.

The moment that I extended my hand to receive this certificate, I was so happy and tears of joy and gratitude to God ran down my face. My life continued to be filled with excitement. As I was becoming older, my God was still blessing me with health. I kept on going and traveling. My next memorable trip was in July 1986, Labor Day weekend to Battle Creek ,Michigan. We visited the historic Adventist village, originally known as "Advent Town." It is the home of James and Ellen White and other Adventist pioneers. The trip by bus from Brooklyn to Battle Creek, Michigan, took as least 12 hours. We left at midnight and arrived late afternoon the next day. When we arrived, my body was numb from sitting down. I took a bath and a quick nap and I was ready to go. I had the privilege of visiting one of the oldest churches, the White's home, and I was able to hold Sister White's Bible, play with the Old Organ, and to touch the printing press, the same press that was used in her first publication of religious literature and health reform literature. I touched the clay, the yellowish and greenish basin, and a pitcher. I also visited the Colleges' Cereal City, the great Adventist academy known today as Andrews University, and the famous Kalamazoo river as well as the burial sites of the White family, and other pioneers.

My plan in life is not even near over. In a few short years I would be celebrating my 80th birthday. "The days of our lives are seventy years; and if by reason of strength they are eighty years; yet their boast is only labor and sorrow; for it is soon cut off, and we fly away," (Psalms 90:10). This is the blessing, that God had promised to mankind. My overall well being was fair for someone who was about to reach the peak of longevity. Physically my body was very strong, except that my eyes were bothering me. I visited the optometrist's office for complete vision examinations, and later learned that I had a cataract on my right eye.

In the early 1987, I visited the eye specialist for a follow up on the first diagnosis of my cataract, but I was advised that it would be best to wait until the cataract had covered the entire eye. On my way from the doctor's office, I met one of my coworker. We were glad to see each other after over 15 years. Her name was Geneva. She told me about a trip that she was planning a trip to Hawaii in the summer, and if I was willing to go. Naturally, my response was in the affirmative manner. I had always dreamed of going to Hawaii, where the TV Series Hawaii 5-0 was filmed. The price was right, the time was appropriate, and right away I saw it as a golden opportunity for me to visit, and was not going to let it pass by. I told her that I was going to let my children know about the trip, and I would get back to her. We exchanged telephones numbers. Two days later, I got in touch with Geneva, and I told her to include Mina and myself for the 10 day trip. Hawaii is as beautiful as it is seen in pictures, and on TV. Hawaii is a breathtaking island. In describing it, I can only compare it with the description that we have heard about the Garden of Eden. If there is a place on this earth as beautiful as Hawaii, I imagine that is what the Garden of Eden must be like.

The island grows all kinds and types of flowers, and the beaches are covered with beautiful white sand. The seawater is clear like crystal, any tropical fruits that you can name you can find it there, the hills and mountains are covered with olive green vegetation, and from the top of Diamond Hill, you can admire the entire Hawaiian Islands just laying dormant in the midst of the ocean. We visited many historical sights such as the Shrine that is located where the SS Arizona Ship sank, in the waters of Pearl Harbor. The museum where the names of those who perished in the bombing of Pearl Harbor by the Japanese in 1945 are listed. What was comical about this trip, was that I tried to do the Hawaiian Dance. Just imagine me trying to keep up moving my hips like the Hawaiian ladies, but I gave it my best. Remember that I was not a young chicken, but an old hen, but I still had a lot of stamina. The one that I serve every day has promised to anoint me with the Holy Spirit, and to keep me in a sound mind. By taking care of my body I represent the Temple of the living and loving God.

I am very grateful to God for remembering His humble servant, and wanting not only the good for me, but the very best with a price. Thus was my sole responsibility to strive for. For this reason, I customarily rise early in the morning to breathe the fresh air into my body, and to eat the proper food. Whenever I feel the cool clean air slipping into my body, it makes me feel rejuvenated and ready to go. The air improves my thinking ability, my alertness, and my overall being. Sometimes I say out loud, "what a great way to begin the day with fresh air!" This I believe has been the factor that has contributed to my longevity and my physical strength. I often remember that the Monarch of the Universe is the breathe of life to my soul.

My source of happiness has come from the habits that I have cultivated many years ago.

My happiness is from my spiritual freedom which came for me on September 29, 1958, when I proudly accepted to be baptized, and be called a child of God. I could not have done it without the Lord's Spirit which touched the core of my life. From this day, I discovered freedom from fear of rejection, freedom from the cares of life by believing God's words, "if the Son of God makes you free, you will be free indeed, " (John 8:36). Since I was free spiritually, I had wings to fly.

I returned back to Honduras before the cold weather of 1987 began. Since 1972, I can count the winters that I spent in New York on one hand. When it turned cold, I was always running to the city of refuge, Coxen Hole, with it's temperature in the month of December at 96 degrees. As usual, I knew that my regular job was waiting for me when I returned. As soon as I arrived in Coxen Hole, the news spread and the next thing I knew, people were knocking on my door with a box containing injections. They came from the nearby townships of Spanish Town, French Harbor, Sandy Bay, Grabble Bay, Watering Place,Coconut Garden, and West End.

All of this started when Doctor Polo referred me to some of his patients to give them injections. Dr. Polo was often over burdened with patients, and when he was out of his office, he contacted me and inquired if I would help. This happened many times, and I did not mind helping because I learned that some of these individuals was not sure of what they should believe; they were starving spiritually. I saw this as a good opportunity to talk to them about God, and I realized that God gave me the opportunity to share my belief with the people I was helping. Not only did I tell them about God, but I shared the health reform program, which is an essential part of the Advent message. A strong feeling of responsibility for soul winning to Christ invaded me. Gradually, some of the older individuals were becoming interested in the Holy Word that I shared with them. In the islands we have a big problem keeping a permanent pastor for our church. There is only so much that the members of the church can do to lead the people to God. Not all of those that became interested in what I shared with them fully accepted. I felt that we were missing someone with a theological background that would be able to be more detailed of the Word of God.

At the end of the year, our church always had a Christmas party for the children, and I enjoyed being around them. I know that some may think what pleasure would an elderly woman get being around younger children. Yet I was a woman who gave birth to ten children, and raised nine of them; I was a grandmother of 24 grandchildren and great-grand-mother of 14. Children make me remember when I was raising my children, because I often see similar behaviors in some of these children when I think of my own children; in the way they express themselves, and the way they do certain things. When I was raising my children, it was a difficult task at times to meet all their needs, but I did my best with what I had.

At times I could not afford the things that my children can for their children. When my children were younger, we would collect the cigarette silver raps for months, and make ornaments to hang on the Christmas tree. After the homework was done at night, we gathered around the dinning room table with a bundle of cigarette raps, matches boxes, needle and thread, starch, and scissors, and we made bells, runners, balls, paper dolls, and little houses. It was fun for us to work together, and we would share in the praises our family received from our neighbors for our creations. I am proud to say that my family was the first in our neighborhood to put up a little Christmas tree during the holiday season.

Albert and I both wished to make our children's childhood enjoyable. We didn't always succeed, but we tried. Christmas time and birthdays were celebrated with no more than a pound cake and the music from our old gramophone, yet our children danced and enjoyed themselves with even only one or two close neighbor children. Don't assume our efforts were always appreciated. But I believe that parents can never do too much for their children. Most likely one or two children will rebel and resent one or both parents. God is my judge. I made the best out of the worse situation for my children. Yet, I have been blamed for what I did wrong or what I did not, or what I should have done.

Children don't realize the pain and suffering parents go through raising them, until they too became a parent. I gave God my heart, and prayed prayers of fervent gratitude for my children, and for what He provided for me and them. From my lips, I enthusiastically praised Him for not allowing me to hold a grudge for whatever they might have said about me.

Our church celebrated Christmas with the children by providing food and inexpensive gifts for them, and this made them happy. It was our little way of making the children enjoy the spiritual meaning of Christmas as a gift from God through His Son Jesus Christ our Lord. It was copied by other churches in the community, and we all shared the burden for those less fortunate than others. For the teenagers, we prepared food and gifts. The following years, we invited the children to be a part of a Christmas show. I strongly believed in the children, and I know that they had the power to get things done. We must show them the right example to follow. Even Jesus told His disciple that unless we became as a little child, we have no hope of entering Heaven. Children are humble, and they are honest. These are the qualities the Lord is looking to find in His people. In the Word it says that a person will become a man, and he also will be a child twice in his lifetime, so childhood is a very important stage in the human existence on this earth.

In speaking about children, two days before the New Year 1988, the telephone rang. It was a call from my prodigal child Terrell, living in San Diego, California, and it was the answer to my prayer and deepest dream. For some time, I did not know if he was alive or dead. My first reaction was shock, and I could hardly believe what I was hearing. Terrell was wishing me holiday greetings, and he invited me to attend his graduation from Berkeley Law School on May 30, 1988. I was overwhelmed by the good news. I burst out in tears of joy thanking and praising my Savior. I remember vividly the look on Eduardo's face as he rushed into the living room after hearing me praising God. He looked concerned as he inquired what was happening. I related to him the good news that I had received from Terrell, and he too shared my joy. He had finally began to show some maturity in his life after so many years.

After attending college, he was finally going to make me feel proud of him. He also told me that I was going to be able to meet my grand-daughter, Mirr. I was happy, and like usual, thanking God, because it had been a long time that I not heard from him. The last time I heard from Terrell was in July 1985, when he came to New Orleans for General Conference.

Over the following weeks, I booked my passage on Sahasa Airline with a destination to New Orleans to visit a few weeks with my sisters, and then continued to New York. I had to finish some repairs on my house. It was close to ten years since it was built, and it was more than overdue. At the same time I wanted to eat some of the fruit that was soon to be harvested.

In mid march, when the weather was better, I landed at New Orleans Airport. I immediately called my sister America to pick me up. I discussed my plan with my sisters about going to California, but something came up, and I had to postpone my trip to New York. A close friend and her husband of America had planned to travel to Europe for three weeks to attend a Medical Convention, and on a short notice they were told that the person who had agreed to baby sit for their two children, ages 7 and 9 years old, had an emergency. At first I thought about my trip to New York, and the cold temperatures reported on the news stated that it was still very cold. America took advantage of the situation, and asked me to baby sit for her friends. I accepted, but deep within me I felt that this was all prearranged by my sister. One of my weaknesses had always been children. How could I say no? In the end, I too was benefiting from this situation. I was going to make some extra dollars to add to my retirement check. However, the three weeks turned out to be five weeks. After the couple returned from their trip, America confessed that her hand was deep in this timely planning. I had to laugh about her cleverness.

I called my daughters in New York and told them to meet me in San Diego, California on May 28th. This trip to California was going to be my second one. I had been there before in San Francisco in 1982, to see Terrell's son Jean-John Paul and Jan North his mother. The trip had been worth it. It hurt me to say, that Terrell is the only one of my children that I did not have the pleasure to see mature spiritually, I am still praying for his salvation.

During the time I spent in New Orleans, I only thought about how God had answered another one of my prayers. In my life one of the greatest events was about to take place in a few weeks in San Diego. I had a wonderful time taking care of the children, seeing everybody, and being out with old friends, and making new ones. Finally, the day came for me to travel from New Orleans to San Diego. I was very excited, and felt like I could shout. I was met at the airport by my children, and taken to the hotel, where later on I took a bath and made myself comfortable until I fell asleep for a while. After a few hours of good sleep, and my battery was charged. I felt rejuvenated from my flight, and ready to have some food. This was the third time that I was going through a jet lag experience. My first experience was when I flew to Athens in 1982, and the second to Hawaii in 1987. Before dinner, Terrell brought his son John Paul to pass the weekend with us. The last time I had seen John, he was a toddler, now he was much older. This was the first time for John to see Mina. Sue had seen him when he was a few months old.

The next day, early in the morning on May 30, was a beautiful day. The sun was bright, the sky blue and a cool breeze just sweeping over San Diego. It was "the day" of my life. Terrell's daughter, Mirr, and her mother Michelle came to the hotel to go with us to the graduation ceremony, and to take us to their home for a barbecue after the ceremony. This was the moment that I had long waited for. In a matter of hours, we would attend Terrell's graduation ceremony. My emotional volcano was about throw out it's tears of lava, but I read my Bible in the morning, and prayed for it not to happened. While getting dressed, I thought about the decision I had made many years previously, that with the help of the Almighty, I would try to give my children the opportunity to go to school and build the foundation for their future on. That day I would see how my choice had impacted more than once in the life of another one of my children. In just a few hours, Terrell would soon walk down the isle in an auditorium before many eyes. Proud parents like myself would be there to see our children receive their law degrees.

My photographic memory kicked in before my eyes, and I saw my children from the oldest to the youngest, as they first stepped on the premises of the "Juan Brooks" elementary school, and allowed themselves to go farther in the future. My thoughts also wandered on how God the Creator feels when He see His handy work, his creatures who have been through the school of life, and have graduated; ready to enter His Heavenly Kingdom. I felt like my emotions broke away from my body's internal volcano, and once again tears of joys became rivers of praise. I can surely say that I enjoy reliving the decision that I made earlier in life because it had done it's work; the lives of my children were impacted.

God has created us all with the capacity to make right choices in life. Sometime we fail because of wrong choices, and our lives end up in chaos, and we do not blame ourselves, but others for a wrong decision. I had to recreate that memory that I love to remember, because our memories are our lives. Having my children go further educationally than I was allowed to is one of the greatest achievement of my life. I returned to New Orleans to pick up the rest of my personal belonging, and then returned to New York.

On June 24, 1988, I celebrated my 80th birthday as God had promised. As usual my children, grandchildren and in-laws were there with the traditional cake and cards, and we celebrated my day. I felt stronger than ever and ready to go and conquer the world. I gave God thanks for sparing my life. Now I had only nine more years to live to be as old as Chila and probably Grandma McKay. I had the confidence in God that He was going to allow me to reach that good old age. Even with aches and pains, I was going see my 89th birthday. For the past twenty years plus, I have always celebrated my birthdays in New York with my children since I migrated to the United States in 1966.

Before leaving for Honduras, I had a conversation with Mina, and she told me that she was thinking about Social Work Graduate School in the Fall of 1988. This was another occasion that made me remember my promise years ago that warmed my heart. I encouraged her to go as far as the Good Lord would permit her. She pursued her dreamed until she attended her first class three months later. Around the end of September, I returned to Honduras. I was still feeling good about the events of the past two years, but my tears of joy suddenly changed to sorrow.

In late October I received a call from New York telling me that Olimpia and Dorothy were involved in a car accident in Plantation, Florida, and it was serious. My body froze when I heard the bad news. All kinds of horrible scenes ran through my head. As soon as I hung up the phone, Sister Maud was coming from up town, and she saw me on the front porch. She approached my gate, and asked me what was the matter. I told her the news that I had received. She advised me to pray for my daughter, and to leave everything in God's hands. After I emptied my heart to my creator with Maud, I felt better. I know that I did not have the courage to return to Florida. I feared the worse "death" would happen again in the family, but I found strength in bombarding Heaven's prayer line. Day and night I called out to God in prayer. Despite my human fears of death, there was a deep peace that kept me believing that God was going to see her through the accident, and He did.

My experiences with prayers can fill many deep wells. They have been marvelous. I can't remember when my prayers were not answered as I have petition Heaven. There were those that were delayed, and the answer that came in the opportune time, just when I was giving up. I gave God thanks for my free telephone line with Him, and for the telephone in the house and that I am able to pay the bills. Listening for the telephone became a priority for me until Olimpia was released from the hospital. It kept me in contact with her progress.

In 1989, we had another confrontation with death. I was still in Honduras in February, waiting for the winter to pass so I could come back to New York. It was February 14th, Valentine's Day, when I got the call from New York, informing me about my sister Eloise's sudden death the previous Sunday. When I mentioned sudden death, no death is sudden, because from the moment we come into this world, death is the only thing that is sure to every human life, and the life of every living creature.

It does not matter how often we go through this phase of life, death always hurts; to know that the person we love and care for will not be seen on this earth for a while until the day of the resurrection. So I packed my suitcase again, and booked another flight to New Orleans to attend the burial of Lolo. My three daughter from New York and my oldest son also accompanied me to New Orleans.

After the burial, I remained with America for sometime before returning back to Honduras. I realized that Lolo was gone, so our family had been reduced to three: America, Junior and Me. America was also mourning the lost of her husband, Peter Moret, who had passed away in 1986. We tried to contact Junior in Belize through a friend, Lucille Bennette. She has always been our contact person, but this time she was not able to find Junior. Since I had seen all of my children that year, I decided to return to Honduras. I felt guilty; in just a few weeks June would soon be here, and I would be celebrating another birthday if my life was spared. So I changed my mind, packed my bag, and hit the airway to New York.

As usual, June 24 came and went, and I celebrated another birthday with gifts. One of my presents for the occasion was a Bible with big letters. My eyes were beginning to give me some problems, and I gladly welcome the gift. I had my eyes checked again for the cataract, and was advised that it was ready to be removed. I needed some time to think about it, so I made it a matter of prayer and discussed the surgery with my children. We agreed that I would have the eye surgery after I returned to Honduras for a visit.

In October 1989, I had enough of being in the concrete city, and was ready to go where I would be able to breath pure clean air, and be away from the winter snow and cold. I couldn't wait to return to my homeland, where I was free to enjoy the early morning. I love to get up early and go out to take a walk either to the airport, or on the highway to look over the ridge towards the Tactch point and the ocean. There I stood as the sun's first rays blazed across the horizon, observing the mist on the grass, flowers and feeling the warm sun on my face. I then breathed deeply and flooded my lungs with the fresh cool air. I think about God and thank Him for another new day.

On this trip home, I noticed that the population was continuing to increase since the mid 1980s. It was the result of the ongoing influx of individuals and families from the mainland. Everywhere you went in Coxen Hole, there was a strange face staring at you. These newcomers were from a much lower socioeconomic status, and their lifestyle was much different than what we were used to. Not all of them had an undesirable lifestyle, and only God knew who else was among them. Rumors started to spread that some of these individuals, especially the young single males, were ex-convicts who had served time in prison for murder or robbery.

In a small town bad news spreads very quickly. I feared for my grandchildren who lived with me. Most mothers shared the same feelings. When even a minor crime occurred, such as stealing or fighting, people started to fear that the worse would come and it did come. One day, a mother reported to the authorities that she had some male clothes hanging under her house to dry one night, and the next morning when she got up they were missing. She strongly believed that one of the newcomers had committed the crime. This incident made a lot of people angry, and they united in voicing their fears before the mayor's office. They were told that there was no written laws prohibiting people from the mainland from coming to live on the island, or vice versa.

We were not pleased with the answer to our plight, so we went to the governor's office only to hear the same. We were advised to be more careful in not leaving our windows or doors open, or leaving anything outside that could easily carried away such as tubs, buckets, machetes, axes, etc. Living with such uncertainty is a very scary feeling. People protected their property every evening by making sure their windows were well secured, as well as any lose objects in the yard.

One day our fears grew worse, when a three year old girl was found dead, hanging on a coconut tree on the beach. When her body was examined by the health center, the doctor reported that the child was sexually molested. The case was investigated, but no one was apprehended. The family of the little one had to bear their pain without the culprit being punished for the crime. In all my days, this was the first time for something so cruel to happen in my hometown. I cannot prove that something like this might had not happened before, but it wasn't known to be public. In cases like this, one feels helpless and hopeless in the system that should protect it's citizens.

I realized the we are living in the last days when there will not be any respect for life. The love between one human being and another is being withdrawn, states the Bible. "Love does no harm to another," (Romans 13:10). Satan is having a field day, but it is not going to last for long, because God will intervene on behalf of His believers. God's words are true since the beginning of the world, and He will continue to rule from His throne in Heaven. "For assuredly, I say to you, till heaven and earth pass away, one jot or tittle will by no means pass from the law [word] till all be fulfilled," (Matthew 5:18). By God's grace, I want to remain faithful until that glorious day. I know that He will protect me from all danger and harm that is taking place on the island.

I think the elderly felt especially insecure in our home land, especially on the street at night. The only time that I was out at night was when I was going to Wednesday night prayer meetings and Sunday night services, and I was always accompanied by someone. I remembered when my children were small, some nights we would fall asleep with our doors and windows open, and nothing happened.

One of my greatest fears was for Edward. He had a tendency to walk alone on the street at night. Many nights I could not sleep until he came home, then my mind was at peace. I have lived in New York, and it was natural for one to live with fear because of all the crime that are reported on the television news and radios. Never would I think, that the day would come that my feelings towards this little paradise I called my homeland would have ever changed. Even this generation has changed drastically when compared to when my children were growing up. There is little respect shown among some of the youngsters towards the elderly.

One day I had an encounter with a boy of about six years old. While I sat on my porch, the little boy was climbing on my wire fence. I said to him, "Sonny please get off the fence." His response to me was the big "F...! Do not F... with me, because I do not F... with you!" While he said that to me, he stood there staring at me without blinking a eye. Two gentlemen were standing across the street in front of my house, when they heard the boy's response, and they were surprised as well. They then said to the child if he knew to whom he was speaking, and he replied, "that is Ms. Nana." Then he looked into their faces and said to the men, "I told her not to F... with me!" and then he walked away. These two men's mouths dropped opened from what they had just heard. The first man, Mr. S., said to Mr. P., "In my days, you dared not look at a older person, much less say say to them what we just heard." Such would have been grounds for instant harsh punishment.

Today I realize that some of this generation cannot hold a decent conversation without including a curse word. My grown children will never curse in my presence, and I hope that they will never do it in front of their seniors. I tried to bring them up with a sense of respect for others and self, and so far I have been successful.

Another New year was approaching, and only God knew what was in store for me. I was willing to let Him have His way in my life. One thing I knew was that I had to take the old route to New York, and I planned to do so in the summer to get another eye exam, God's will would be done. I came to New York the last week in July, 1990, to live with Mina who had moved to Bainbridge Street. At first I felt somewhat strange because I was not going back to good old Bushwick Avenue, where I had lived from 1966 to 1989.

Bushwick Avenue holds a lot of good memories for me. I have enjoyed many evenings looking from the window in my apartment on the second floor, down on the ongoing traffic of cars flowing and people passing by. I also enjoyed talking with friends across the street; however I was somewhat familiar with Bainbridge Street because Mt. of Olives SDA Church had been located on Hopkins Street and Bainbridge Street where I used to attend. Prior to it moving to Bushwick Avenue. On Bainbridge Street I had to learned to adjust to the quietness in the neighborhood, but now I enjoyed the peacefulness of the neighborhood. I found out that the people on the block are very friendly, and the most of them were like myself—we had paid our dues, and now were reaping the fruit of our labors. Retirement is wonderful when one knows it is best. When I came to Bainbridge to live, three of my grandsons, Alfonso, Rue and Cromwell, lived in the same building and it helped with my adjustment. I was still surrounded with family, and Perta was still on Bushwick Avenue only a block away.

During an eye examination sometime ago, I was told about a cataract that was growing on my right eye, so I went to the optometrist as a follow up, and was told that the cataract had ripped and it should be removed as soon as possible. I was aware that my eyesight was getting worse, because I had difficulty reading which has been one of my leisure time habits. At first I had hoped that something else could be done, maybe some special medical treatment, but to my amazement, surgery was the only treatment for cataracts.

CHAPTER 20

In 1990, two weeks after arriving in New York, I had an appointment with the optometrist. The result of this visit was that my eye had remained the same, and surgery again was recommended. An appointment for surgery was made for the end of September. I thank God that all went well despite the constant eye drops that were required every four hours for two weeks, when it was reduced to every eight hours.

The healing process of the eye was a success, and I was able to see better. For sometime I was not able to indulge in reading the Holy Word for any length of time. Reading the Word of God is my number one habit. It has been successful in my Christian life, along with my daily talk to God, before talking to another human. Every day I want to be on God's side. I know that if I fail to read and pray for knowledge, help and strength from God to overcome temptations, I know that my day is going to be a bad one. I do not want to go astray spiritually.

As my right eye continue to heal, I was ready to go, but started to have some problems seeing through my left eye. I think it began to empathize with the other eye. Maybe it too wanted some attention. The left eye was becoming envious of the right. Envy is a dangerous thing, because one never knows what to expect.

In 1992 I had a surprise, when I visited the eye doctor's office and I was told that the left eye's cataract was soon to be ready for removal. I thought about the news, and decided that I wanted to get it over. I was scheduled a date for laser surgery to remove the cataract. That what I mean when I say envy is dangerous. Soon I would have to repeat the eye drops hourly into my eye.

My God never left me alone in the midst of my health problems. He brought me some joy. On June 3, 1992, I attended Mina's graduation from the Hunter Graduate School of Social Work along with Perta, Tomas and Daisy. This event helped me to take my mind off myself, and to praise God for His blessing to be able to see another fruit of my labor before my good eye. A week after Mina's graduation, I packed my bags, and with Sue we returned to Roatan. Sue had a good time as usual, and I always hate to see my children leave. This was the first time in many years that I spent my birthday in Roatan. I stayed home for the balance of the year, and looking forward to celebrate my next birthday with my children in New York.

In mid-spring 1993, I was back in New York, and scheduled for the laser surgery at the Kings Highway Hospital, but it was not successful as the first surgery. Envy is dangerous; the day of the surgery, in the middle of the procedures, something unforeseen happened. The pressure in my eye went up and blood started to flow, making it impossible for the doctor to continue with the surgery. Immediately my eye was bandaged up, and I was taken to the recovery room for a few hours, with some bottles of antibiotic eye drops. They were to be administered at different hours. Two of them every three hours and one medication every eight hours. This intensive treatment went on for three months. In the interim, I had an appointment every week to make sure that the problem was taken care off

During this ordeal, I had concern about my eyesight. It is a scary thing not to know what is going to be the result. I agonized before God in prayer; claiming His blessings earnestly. It was a spiritual warfare I was wresting with God to heal my eye. The earnestness, persistency, and fervency of my praying was for me to reach up to God and for Him to reach down to me. I realized that my petition had to be in proportion to the worth and need of that for which I prayed. I needed to see from this eye and I knew that God was going to intervene. I felt sure that I would receive an answer immediately, but it took a while. I learned that one of the most effective ways for an answer from God is to submit to His will, and then the gate of Heaven is opened to our prayer. When I was fearful, I went to Him, and He spoke peace to the tumults of my soul.

Our God is a loving, willing God, who is infinitely more willing to grant the longing of His children's hearts than any earthly parent would do. He only requires of us to, "Ask and it shall be given you, seek, and ye shall find; knock, and it shall be opened unto you. For every one that asketh recevieth and he that seeketh findeth; and to him that knocketh it shall be opened," (Luke 11:9, 10). It should be our highest privilege to walk, to live and to talk with Jesus now. It is the responsibility of each one who has a personal experience with Jesus. In doing so, every one of us should be able to say, "I know whom, and I know the Good shepherd, which is Jesus Christ our Savior, and Lord."

I have found in my life that one of my greatest spiritual needs is to cultivate the consciousness of the Divine presence. It is a hard struggle, but possible to overcome, if we just keep our eyes on Jesus. He is the true and only door to the Kingdom of God. But as sinner, when we are in trouble we often turn to another like ourselves, instead of turning to Jesus, who is our mediator between God and man. The Holy Word says, "For there is one God, and one mediator between God and man, the Man Christ Jesus," (1 Timothy 2:5). I held onto my belief that everything was going to be alright, but during a visit to the doctors office he confirmed my belief by assuring me that within six months to a year, he would have to re-operate on my left eye. I would often meet with a friend who would say, that they either knew a relative or friend who had a similar problem with their eye, and after the second try it worked out fine. Their statement reassured my confidence in the doctor's ability to complete his job. I was scheduled in the fall of 1993 to be admitted to Long Island Hospital in Long Island, for the second surgery. I went to the hospital on Monday evening because the surgery was on Tuesday, and I was discharged two days later to start with the three hour eye drop procedure once again.

By now you may have observed that one of my weaknesses is to travel. This year, my traveling was going to be limited to no further than Florida to spend the winter, just in case anything went wrong with my eye. I believe in the role that the doctors play in the health profession. Some of them do not realized that they are in collaboration with God in restoring health.

In 1993, my health begin to fail. I started to feel pain in my legs usually in the morning when I get up from my bed, or sometime when I sit for a long time, I also felt some discomfort in other parts of this tired body of mine, but I thank God every day for His tender mercies. I know that my God has the power to heal all the pain that I might be subjected to. I thought about Chila and the many elderly people, how they might have felt when aches and pain invaded their bodies. They must have experienced what I am feeling now.

Sometimes we do not want to accept the reality of life and just want to continue, like everything is fine, but there comes a time when we have to listen to our bodies. I realized that my time had come for me to listen to what my body was telling me. Nana, it is time to slow down. For more than eighty years plus, I had been on the run, and now the crucial decision in my life has to be made. Whether I want to remain the balance of my days in New York or did I want to go back home to Honduras? Mentally, I knew that I will have to choose what is right for me and my children since, I am still able to travel, but not alone. I will have to depend on one of my children to travel with me. I am willing to schedule my trips around their availability to do so. This year my children and I made a decision to apply for some home attendance service for me, to have someone to be with me while my daughter was at work. I did not feel comfortable having someone staying with me, but because I needed the eye drops so frequently that I had no other choice but to go alone with the service.

My experience with some of the individuals involved in my care was pleasant, mainly the visiting nurse that came to see me. But some of the home attendance ladies were unpleasant. Some of them only wanted to sit down and watch television. I thank God that my children were always calling to make sure that everything went well during the day. I believed that if it were not for their calls, it might not have gone well with me. Other ladies showed that they cared for my well being. They were always asking if I needed anything, and my medication and food was always on time.

I want to share one of my most terrifying experiences with a young lady. I caught her smoking in the bathroom. She was very tall compared to me, as I was only five feet one inch in height. When I found her in the bathroom, she gave me a threatening look, and it made me scared. That evening when my daughter came home, the home care agency was contacted, and we made a request for another lady to come the next day. We were not sure what would happen next in the house with me alone and this person. I met one visiting nursing who came from Florida. This was a very beautiful person. She also invited me to visit her when I went to Florida to see my family. God was with me every step of my life and my family. That was a blessing that many elderly people do not share. I can only imagine what happened to those elderly people who live alone and no relatives near by. It is scary just to think about it. My heart goes out to them, and it brings back memories of what I saw take place in the nursing home where I worked. Some of the elderly people were physically neglected, verbally and physically abused by some of the staff. This is my greatest fear that I might have to go to a nursing home and I would have to physically experience what I saw. I would prefer going back to Honduras and die there, than to go to one of these homes in New York. I pray to the Creator, that my children would not be so cruel to go against my wish and force me to be placed in an institution in a nursing home.

My traveling days alone were coming to an end. On December 10, 1993, Mina and I traveled to Roatan just in time to escape the numerous storms that winter. In Honduras we had a bad winter too, a lot of rain and flood. It was bad for me because my house was being repaired and the rain and flood hindered the progress. It had been many years since 1976, when we had experienced a winter like this in Honduras. Both Christmas Day and New Years Day, all the streets in Coxen Hole were flooded, and the water was up to an average person's knee.

In my yard and under my house, the water was even higher than in the street because they recently fixed the street and did not scrape them before adding more filling to them. Still, I was happy to be home despite all the inconveniences. The hardest moments for me was January 10, 1994, the day that my daughter had to return to New York after we were together for a month. I had a heavy heart, but God knows that I would never stand between my children and their life. I planned to be back in New York in the summer and then to Florida to spend sometime with my other daughter and family and then travel back to no other place but Roatan.

In 1995, while I planning to come to New York, I stopped in Florida and then proceed to New York. One of my grandsons, Wade, gave me a surprise for mother's Day with a beautiful flowered dress. I loved this dress because of the good thought that goes behind it. Wade is my only grandson who seemed to care what I wore. My other grandsons shared gifts such as cards for birthdays, Mother's Day, Christmas, or New Year's day. They all shared their love in different ways to which I am grateful to God for. I do not have enough words to express my gratitude for all of my family.

On November 7–9, 1995, I had a new spiritual experience attending the "It Is Written" yearly partnership weekend. I enjoyed each moment of it. This experience added to my overall life experience, and made me to think about how my lifetime of sin was gone in an instant, the moment I accepted Christ as my Savior. Ever since, I had a zeal to let others know about what I have found; the peace and tranquility in The Word of God, and the inspiring hymns of old. They are comforting and soothing to my soul, and they brought me throughout my life, and awakened the consciousness of my union with my Lord.

Despite all that I have been through in life thus far, death and birth, poverty and prosperity, and suffering and joy, I always get an uplift heavenward when the words of one of these old hymns is sung. I have one hymn that has always been on my mind, and I believed strongly in the words of this hymn; I love this hymn very much for what it has done to me. This hymn is entitled, "Blessed Assurance Jesus is Mine." We must remember that true assurance requires much more than physical blessings, good health, raiment, plenty to eat, and a place to stay. In this life there are individuals that have all of these blessings, and are still miserable. Soul longing cannot be supplied by material things, only in God can one's life have complete spiritual satisfaction.

At times I wonder, if I am going to be alive when my Savior returns. I sure would like to have the experience in being taken up into the clouds to the Holy City, in the New Jerusalem. This earth cannot last much longer because of all the evil that is rampaging through this planet. The Bible says that God will cut time short to save His elect people. By His grace I want to see His face.

We invite you to view the complete
selection of titles we publish at:

www.TEACHServices.com

Scan with your mobile
device to go directly
to our website.

or write or email us your praises,
reactions, or thoughts about this
or any other book we publish at:

TEACH Services, Inc.
P U B L I S H I N G
www.TEACHServices.com

P.O. Box 954
Ringgold, GA 30736

info@TEACHServices.com

TEACH Services, Inc., titles may be purchased in bulk for
educational, business, fund-raising, or sales promotional use.
For information, please e-mail

BulkSales@TEACHServices.com

Finally, if you are interested in seeing
your own book in print, please contact us at

publishing@teachservices.com

We would be happy to review your manuscript for free.